The Pilgrim

1. Intro (:25 instrumental)
2. Sometimes the Pleasure's Worth the Pain (3:10)
3. The Pilgrim (Act I) with Emmylou Harris (:54)
4. Harlan County with Ralph Stanley and the Clinch Mountain Boys (1:32)
5. Reasons with Pam Tillis (3:31)
6. Love Can Go To… (:31)
7. Red, Red Wine and Cheatin' Songs with Pam Tillis (3:11)
8. Truckstop with George Jones, Emmylou Harris and Earl Scruggs (1:27)
9. Hobo's Prayer (3:37)
10. Goin' Nowhere Fast (3:10)
11. The Observations of a Crow (5:27)
12. Intermission with Ralph Stanley and the Clinch Mountain Boys (:31 instrumental)
13. The Greatest Love of all Time (3:29)
14. The Greatest Love of all Time Reprise (1:54 instrumental)
15. Draggin' Around These Chains of Love (3:13)
16. The Pilgrim (Act II) (:37)
17. Redemption (1:49)
18. The Pilgrim (Act III) (6:04)
19. Outro (Sir Galahad) with Johnny Cash (2:23)
20. Mr. John Henry, Steel Driving Man with Earl Scruggs (2:00 instrumental)

Bonus Tracks / A Traveler's Companion

21. The Pilgrim, Act IV (unreleased alternate take) with Ralph Stanley and the Clinch Mountain Boys, Emmylou Harris, and Connie Smith (1:21)
22. That'll Be All Right with Me (unreleased) with the Rock & Roll Cowboys (2:55)
23. Been Lonely Too Long (unreleased *Pilgrim* project demo) (3:03)
24. I Think We're in Texas (unreleased) with Manuel and Emmylou Harris (0:21)
25. Shout Little Lulie (unreleased) with Ralph Stanley and the Clinch Mountain Boys (2:03 instrumental)
26. Call and Response (unreleased) with Uncle Josh Graves (0:40)
27. Evelina (unreleased) with Uncle Josh Graves (1:25 instrumental)
28. Tennessee Wagoner (unreleased) with Earl Scruggs, Stuart Duncan (1:58 instrumental)
29. Even Trains Have to Cry (unreleased *Pilgrim* project demo) with The Fabulous Superlatives (3:36)
30. The Vanishing (unreleased *Pilgrim* project demo) (1:31 instrumental)

the pilgrim

A WALL-TO-WALL ODYSSEY

MARTY STUART

Photography by Jim Arndt

the pilgrim

A WALL-TO-WALL ODYSSEY

MARTY STUART

BMG

MARTY STUART'S CONGRESS OF COUNTRY MUSIC

Design by Karen Cronin, Cronin Creative

Cover photography by Jim Arndt
Back cover photography by Helen Frances Burt Allen, Nashville, Tennessee, October 1934

Library of Congress Cataloging-in-Publication Data available upon request.

ISBN: 9781947026506

Published by BMG
www.bmg.com

Contents

B.T.P. (before the Pilgrim)

MARTY STUART
the pilgrim

Preface

In the same way the Bible is divided into the Old and New Testaments, Marty Stuart's musical career is divided into everything that came before 1999 and everything that came after. The dividing line is *The Pilgrim*, Stuart's tenth studio album. The risky and ambitious concept project—based on true events that transpired in his hometown of Philadelphia, Mississippi—was a turning point in Marty's unique artistry. While not a commercial success at the time, *The Pilgrim* represents a rediscovery of his roots and a creative rebirth that continues to reverberate today as we celebrate the album's twentieth anniversary.

From the art direction, to the eccentric narrative, to the participation of iconic performers such as Earl Scruggs, Ralph Stanley, George Jones, Johnny Cash, Emmylou Harris, and Connie Smith, *The Pilgrim* somehow managed to connect with the deepest spirit of country music's rich traditions while also breaking new ground.

It's impossible to understand Marty Stuart without understanding what led to *The Pilgrim* and how it has shaped who he is today as an uncompromising artist and an unflinching evangelist for pure country music. Presented here is the original album, unreleased bonus material, and a close look at its development and continuing influence.

Scott B. Bomar
Author/Music Historian
Los Angeles, California

Foreword

I suppose you could call *The Pilgrim* the hillbilly *Tommy* or the country version of a Roger Waters concept album. Or you could compare it to Willie Nelson's *Redheaded Stranger*. Those are all good things to be compared to, but this is its own animal.

First of all, Marty Stuart is known predominantly as a country singer, country songwriter, and country musician, and he has excelled at all that. However, I've known Marty a long time, we've had a lot of late night talks, and we've worked together quite a lot. What people may not know about Marty is his deep knowledge of all kinds of music and his love and knowledge of storytelling. He has as much respect for rock and roll, rhythm and blues, jazz, and pretty much every other kind of music as he does for country, gospel, and bluegrass.

The songs on *The Pilgrim* are soulful and well crafted (as usual for a Marty record), but it's pointless to go into a song-by-song analysis, because it should be listened to as a whole piece. It's a story set to music. The music and the story are a beautiful marriage. It's haunting, both lyrically and sonically. Marty has taken a real-life story and put it in the form of a Southern Gothic opera. He's joined by excellent musicians, who bring their own souls into it and make the characters breathe in a uniquely dynamic way.

Marty knows the value and the musical rhythmic nature of great movies and great novels. He isn't just the greatest mandolin player we have; he's a storyteller in the tradition of Erskine Caldwell, John Steinbeck, Tennessee Williams, and William Faulkner.

Unfortunately, most great artists' finest work is usually overshadowed by their commercial work. If you want to hear a masterpiece, forget about dancing for an hour and listen to Marty Stuart's *The Pilgrim*.

Billy Bob Thornton
Los Angeles, California

Photography by Anthony Scarlati

One can begin to get a sense of *who Marty Stuart is* from his photographs and writings in this book. For a closer look, here's a clue: Marty Stuart is authentic. By that, I mean everything he does, thinks, or imagines comes from *who he is*—not who some people might think he is. Marty knows *who he is* and, because of that, his integrity is naturally a part of him.

He is a consummate musician coming from *who he is*. He has an artist's eye when he looks through the lens of his camera or enjoys the work of others. His writings are those of a poet.

So, who *is* Marty Stuart? Speaking only from my personal experience of him, he is a *blessing*. He has blessed me by giving new meaning and new life to my fifty plus years of work, which is now being cared for by the Museum at the University of Mississippi at Oxford. The work will now have an educational function long after the time of its creation. That is the legacy. That is *who Marty Stuart is* and what he has given to me.

Beyond that, he has touched my heart and enriched my soul—and that is immeasurable.

Thomas B. Allen
Illustrator/Educator
Sarasota, Florida

Marty Stuart is the last link to the original greats of country music. Unlike his contemporaries, he didn't just bring traditional country music of the '50s and '60s back to a younger audience. He has always been a part of it—since he started playing for Lester Flatt as a child. Most importantly, the vibrancy and excitement of Marty Stuart playing live highlights him in the middle of what, according to F. Scott Fitzgerald, is the most elusive act of American careers—the second act. He's an artist who has made it through the storms and the ups and downs of a life spent in music. He has accomplished a real second act by making great, new, relevant music, performed with skill and passion in front of excited audiences, without making any concessions to mainstream or "commercial" fads and trends.

Gandulf Hennig
Filmmaker
Fillmore, California (2019)

Marty Stuart Archives

"*The Pilgrim* is a fabulous journey." - JOHNNY CASH

"The Pilgrim is one part musical, one part parable, one part tribute, and one part shot at redemption." - *NO DEPRESSION*

"This album proves Marty Stuart is the keeper of the hillbilly flame." - EMMYLOU HARRIS

"This record is perfect. I can't quit playing it. Now we see what Marty really wants to do and who he is. It defies all categories. I wish critics weren't allowed to listen to it. This is pure, honest, beautiful art and shouldn't ever be commented on by anyone other than the kind who made it." - BILLY BOB THORNTON

"Stuart carves a masterwork of country styles into each song, all of them performed with a spirit and flair that's uncommon in anything that passes for country music these days.... *The Pilgrim* works because Stuart has country music in his heart." - *THE AUSTIN CHRONICLE*

"Stuart exploits all of his loves and talents—bluegrass, honky-tonk, country-rock—to explore the heights and depths of the human experience." - MICHAEL MCCALL, *THE NASHVILLE SCENE*

"This is an amazing album."- DON WAS

"The most artistically cohesive and rewarding such work since Willie Nelson's 1975 opus, *Red Headed Stranger*." - *BILLBOARD*

"He has absorbed and cultivated every strain of music that ever stirred a hillbilly soul. And now, all that teaching and experience has been poured into *The Pilgrim*, a record that transcends anything he's ever done."- CRAIG HAVIGHURST, *COUNTRY MUSIC*

"*The Pilgrim* is a fascinating look back at country music's past and perhaps a peek into country's future." - *COUNTRY WEEKLY*

"Marty Stuart seems wrapped in his destiny at this point in time. Not only as country music's most notable ambassador/caretaker, but as its main archetypical crusader. He has without question evolved into one of the most important roots musicians and visionaries in America." - PETER NORTH

"Stuart tells the story perfectly, utilizing creaky Appalachian vocal dust, crackling bluegrass, twangy honky tonk, plus tasty rock and string arrangements."
- LOS ANGELES DAILY NEWS

"When I think of country music I think of Marty Stuart. He is that Pilgrim. There is Marty then there is everyone else of his generation. What sets Marty apart is he embodies his culture, he is the go-to man for country music, say the way Louis Armstrong or Miles Davis were for jazz. Marty is my brother. We see things in a universal, common clarity."
– WYNTON MARSALIS

"This concept album about cheating, suicide and redemption is as Gothic as country gets."- BRIAN MANSFIELD, *USA TODAY*

"What a story. This is my idea of country music. This record astounds me."- STEPHEN KING

"Gone is the party-hearty country-rock of Stuart's previous records. In its place is a tapestry that stretches across a century's worth of Americana, from old-time music and bluegrass to blues and honky-tonk."- BILL FRISKICS-WARREN, *THE WASHINGTON POST*

"His writing has never been more lyrical."- ALANNA NASH, *ENTERTAINMENT WEEKLY*

"Here are the great themes of hillbilly music—infidelity, violence, rambling, alcoholism, church and family—wrapped up in an ongoing narrative. It's not surprising that Stuart can get satisfying results from this material when he reaches back to older musical styles and such guest performers as Ralph Stanley, George Jones, Johnny Cash, and Earl Scruggs. More impressive is the way he makes the same themes work with the cranked-up, drum-driven country-rock of modern Nashville, which seems to have forgotten how gripping the dark side of human drama can be." - GEOFFREY HIMES

"*The Pilgrim*, a 'concept' album by Marty Stuart that you could, with equanimity, call the country music version of Sgt. Pepper…has depth, range, and passion; you couldn't shake it if you wanted to."- *OXFORD AMERICAN*

"*The Pilgrim* is an ambitious concept album—a song cycle, really—about love, guilt, alcoholism, death and redemption."- *LOS ANGELES TIMES*

Introduction

The Pilgrim is a record I dearly love. This recording changed the course of my musical life. Year after year, since its original release in 1999, I've heard stories from people all around the world about how *The Pilgrim* made its way into their lives and touched their hearts.

I had to make this record in order to live with myself. At the time of its creation, all my efforts in the booming country music parade of the 1990s had pretty much run their course. I needed a change. I longed for artistic growth and spiritual expansion. I was hungry for a broader task, something that was definitive, epic, monumental. At the same time, I felt the need to reconnect with the roots of my musical raising.

I'd grown accustomed to the near-impossible task of straddling the worlds of old and new country music. I was raised in one, living in another. I had carried many of the customs, sounds, and pageantry from the old world into the modern age, always mindful of the lessons I'd learned while growing up in Lester Flatt's and Johnny Cash's bands. Innovation was always strived for, though somehow I'd lately found myself to be a crooked arrow always landing just shy of the mark. Even with such a storied pedigree, I somehow managed to wind up in the middle of nowhere, in the weeds, a weary-hearted figure, frayed by the rough side of the scramble for fame and fortune. I was a house divided, and something had to give.

The Pilgrim project was the first step in a journey that led me to the outer edge of the awakenings of my true musical heart and soul. *The Pilgrim* also took me back to the bedrock of my upbringing, where the shadows of my mentors loomed large and cast an eternal glow. During this gust of change, the past, present, and future seemed to harmonize and glow, and an air of newness was all around.

While I was developing *The Pilgrim*, I sought vision. I made a number of trips to visit and play music with people I love and admire, whom I consider to be divine sources of inspiration. I looked for wisdom at every turn while continuing to gather the courage to follow my heart into the unknown.

As I wrote and eventually recorded the songs, I knew *The Pilgrim* would forever stand as a personal victory. I also believed critics, scholars, and serious music lovers would give the project consideration. However, in my heart of hearts, I suspected that after presenting the project to my record label, the drive back home from Nashville's Music Row would be a very lonely stretch of road.

I'd be lying if I said a piece of me didn't break when this record was passed over and kicked to the side when it was released. It hurt. I couldn't quite figure out what to do with all my pain until I thought of calling upon a fountain of infinite wisdom. I dialed 615-822-5615, and John R. Cash picked up the phone. I told him I needed to talk with him about something that was bothering me. He said, "C'mon." I drove to his house, and over a glass of iced tea, I shared my disappointment with him. He listened to my story and then said, "I can relate. I wish you could have gone with me to Columbia Records when I delivered *A Day in the Grand Canyon with Johnny Cash,* which was just me walking around the Grand Canyon with a tape recorder, talking about things I was seeing that I found interesting. Or when I turned in my eight-song *Bitter Tears* album, which spit out the truth of the white man's injustice toward the American Indian. I was extremely proud of those projects, but the record company had no idea what to do with those records, or especially me at the time."

J. R. then asked, "Are you proud of your work on *The Pilgrim*?" I said, "Yes I am." He asked, "Would you do it again now, knowing the full consequences?" I answered, "In a heartbeat." He set his glass of tea on the table and said, "Well, son, there's your answer." I said, "Yes sir, thank you." I thought the conversation had ended. J. R. then stood and, in that Johnny Cash voice of the ages, proclaimed, "Your Pilgrim record will come back around someday. I'll assure you! When that time comes, you might find that the record company you're telling me you are likely to be dropped from doesn't exist anymore. The executives who are dismissing you may no longer be regarded as powerful men, and many of the projects which were favored over *The Pilgrim* will have vanished and will be long forgotten." As usual, J. R. was right on all counts.

Going into my archives to search out Pilgrim-related material for this release was like reaching into a dusty old treasure chest. I found songs that I'd written and forgotten, photographs I never got around to looking at, unfinished recordings from *The Pilgrim* sessions, and a string of archival recordings with Earl Scruggs, Johnny Cash, Ralph Stanley & the Clinch Mountain Boys, Emmylou Harris, Connie Smith, and Uncle Josh Graves that I made while they were doing their parts on *The Pilgrim*. Upon listening, those recordings stand as cherished, sacred documents of American roots music that have waited nobly in the shadows for their invitation onto the world stage of the twenty-first century. So many life lessons were offered in the creative process of making *The Pilgrim*. Perhaps the toughest of them all was letting go when the record was considered unsuccessful. However, in letting go, I learned that some things do, in fact, come back around.

Photography by David McClister

Time has been a keeper and an ally of this project. I'm glad *The Pilgrim* has found a home on the north side of the twenty-first century. It feels like an old friend is back in town.

Marty Stuart – 2019

KODAK 5063 TX
COVER
JIM ARNDT SESSION
NEW

MEMPHIS

Photograph by Mike Copelin

706 Union Avenue, Memphis, TN

Photography by Marty Stuart

Memphis, Tennessee is a cool, soulful southern town where the fragrances of magnolias and gardenias get up on the breeze and politely make their way along the boulevards that run throughout the city. The place known as the "home of the blues" pulled me under one if its patented blue-water spells on the hellishly hot summer day of August 22, 1996, as my black Cadillac and I rolled into town. For me, entering Memphis always seemed like passing through the stately gates of a grand biblical city. There was a slow burn hovering above the asphalt of the streets that must have had those old roads begging for mercy, roads that had seen it all, yet say nothing, keepers of a million secrets.

A restless feeling loomed inside me as the sun began to set. I felt the rhythm of the evening trains as they were leaving the Johnson Yard Roundhouse. I heard the voice of the Mississippi River beckoning me to follow along, promising to usher me to a higher caliber of freedom. A choir of crickets along with all of this cosmic bidding wrapped in 102 degrees of Old South heat greeted me as I stepped out of my car onto the sidewalk in front of Sun Records at 706 Union Avenue.

I had booked Sun Studio for two nights to record with my band, the Rock & Roll Cowboys. The reason for the late afternoon arrival was that we couldn't set up our gear and begin to play music until after 6 p.m., when the last of the daily tours was completed. It was understood that everything had to be packed up at the end of the night and set aside in order to make way for the next day's busloads of tourists. Once they were gone, we'd set everything back up

Photography by Marty Stuart

again. The schedule was hard on our crew, but I loved the idea of working at Sun Studio after dark because when it comes to music, Memphis is a night town. Mysterious, unexplainable things happen at night in "Memphisto." Things such as Howlin' Wolf's otherworldly "Moaning at Midnight" and Elvis Presley's masterpiece "Mystery Train," both of which were products of night sessions.

If I'm looking for a new groove, Memphis is a place I return to time and time again. One of my favorite visits was in 1985 as a member of Johnny Cash's band, to participate in a project called *Class of '55* sessions. Cash, Jerry Lee Lewis, Roy Orbison, and Carl Perkins came home to Memphis and Sun Studio to make this "event" record and to film an accompanying television special.

For a week, the city was electrified by the presence of these four men and their entourages, as well as drive-by visits from rock stars, movie stars, and other assorted dignitaries.

Without question, the most charismatic character in the proceedings was Sun Records' founder and lifetime Executive Producer Emeritus to Presley, Cash, Lewis, Orbison, and Perkins, the honorable Sam C. Phillips. I called him Uncle Sam. At one point during the week, I talked with Sam and told him I thought I was ready to start a band and break out

Photography by Dave Darnell, *Commercial Appeal*, Memphis

Class of '55 Sessions at Sun Studio: Johnny Cash, Roy Orbison, Jerry Lee Lewis, Carl Perkins, Chips Moman (hidden), with Marty Stuart and Sam C. Phillips

Photography by Dave Darnell, *Commercial Appeal*, Memphis

Class of '55 Recording Sessions at Sun Studio, clockwise from left: Marty Stuart, Carl Perkins, Bobby Emmons, Bobby Wood, Mike Leech, Reggie Young, Dick Clark crew cameraman

Photography by Dave Darnell, *Commercial Appeal*, Memphis

Carl Perkins presenting Marty Stuart with his Fender Stratocaster guitar at the end of the *Class of '55* Sessions at Sun Studio.

Photography by Dave Darnell, *Commercial Appeal*, Memphis

Class of '55 Recording Sessions at Sun Studio: Cowboy Jack Clement, Marty Stuart, and Johnny Cash

Photography by Dave Darnel, *Commercial Appeal*, Memphis

Class of '55 Recording Sessions at American Sound Studios: "Big Train From Memphis" finale - Marty Stuart, Dave Edmunds, Carl Perkins, and Ricky Nelson

Photography by Dave Darnell, *Commercial Appeal*, Memphis

Photography by Gary C. Earhart, D.D.S.

Left: *Class of '55* Recording Sessions at Sun Studio: Marty Stuart and Jerry Lee Lewis
Above: Class of '55 Recording Sessions at Sun Studio, Jerry Lee Lewis, Carl Perkins, Marty Stuart, Johnny Cash, and Roy Orbison

Rock & Roll Cowboys at Sun Studio: Gary Hogue and Marty Stuart

Photography by Mike Copelin

Rock & Roll Cowboys at Sun Studio: Marty Stuart, Steve Arnold, and Gary Hogue

Photography by Mike Copelin

Photography by Hilda Stuart

on my own. He asked, "What does Johnny think?" I told him he was supportive of the idea. When Sam heard that, he offered his encouragement as well. He told Carl Perkins about our conversation. At the end of the *Class of '55* sessions, Carl gave me his guitar on which he had inscribed, "This box has some hit songs in it, and you're just the cat to get them out of it."

Eleven years later, I'd found some of those hits, which helped me accomplish the first round of what I had set out to do in 1985. Coming full circle, I'd returned to the same inspirational spot at 706 Union Avenue, looking for yet another wave of magic. One of the many beauties of that little studio is its unbridled curiosity. Music can be explored there without fear of consequence. As mighty as the legacy of that room may be, anything new is welcomed with open arms. Sam Phillips designed it that way and his philosophy continues to echo through the ages. Sam opened the doors of the place, inviting all manner of musical possibilities to come in, ultimately providing a setting that was safe and inspirational for musical souls in search of the authenticity buried within. That was exactly what I was looking for.

I booked those two evenings at Sun Studio without having anything definite to record. The first night we laid down a couple of songs we'd been flirting with at some of our sound checks out on the road. There was Jody Reynolds's hypnotic "Endless Sleep" and a truck-driving song called "I'm Coming Home." It's not my nature to call a session without some original songs to record, but I felt if I'd follow my heart to Memphis, a song would appear.

It happened around 6:30 p.m. on the second day. I received a call from my friend, Tony Conway, who was Bill Monroe's manager, giving me word that Mr. Monroe had passed away. Tony asked if I could come back to Nashville and play at his memorial service. The news shook me. I called a break and took a walk around the streets of the Sun Studio neighborhood. I didn't want anyone to see me

Photography by Bill Thorup

Above: Heber Springs, Arkansas, October 1972
Right: Bill Monroe and Marty Stuart radio taping, Music Row, Nashville

Rock & Roll Cowboys,
left to right: Brad Davis,
Steve Arnold, Gary Hogue,
Gregg Stocki, and Marty Stuart

Photography by Bill Thorup

cry. I loved that old man. He had been a presence in my life since I was twelve years old. The first time I met him, he gave me his mandolin pick and told me to take it home and learn how to use it. I carried it everywhere I went for a long time. I didn't show it to anyone or talk about it. That pick was my secret. It was a treasure from a world apart from ordinary hometown life, a world that I longed to be a part of. I believed if Bill Monroe thought enough of me to hand me his mandolin pick, he must have seen something in me that suggested I could play music. And that empowered me.

Not having Bill Monroe around was going to take some getting used to. As I began to walk, I tried to cry, but not one tear would come. I sang his songs, danced, and prayed, but my heart wouldn't speak. I reminisced, thinking of the stories told to me by the old-timers about all those years when Monroe's bluegrass music was dead and generally neglected by the public. Bill Monroe, and whatever musicians he might pick up along the way, would sometimes play for as little as one hundred dollars. However, even though the world had left him cold, the old man stayed true to his vision. I tried to imagine how lonesome life must have been for him while he struggled to survive, and I heard myself say

I am a lonesome pilgrim far from home
And what a journey I have known
I might be tired and weary, but I am strong
Pilgrims walk, but not alone

SUN STUDIO | MEMPHIS, TN

Photographs by Marty Stuart

Rock & Roll Cowboys at Sun Studio, Memphis. Clockwise, from top left: Brad Davis, guitar; Steve Arnold, bass; Gary Hogue, steel guitar; Gregg Stocki, drums

Those four lines unlocked a storm of emotions inside me. I wrote two more verses in my head on the walk back to the studio. By the time I returned to 706 Union Avenue, I had the song written. I went to my mandolin, then told Gregg Stocki, Steve Arnold, Brad Davis, Gary Hogue, and our engineer, James Lott, "This song is in the key of D, it's lonesome, and it's for Bill Monroe. Let's just feel our way through it." The lights were dimmed in the studio, and we recorded "The Pilgrim" in one take. That first version of "The Pilgrim" clocked in at almost ten minutes. We just took our time and journeyed into outer space. When the lights came up, I think all of us sensed that something special had just happened. I went into the control room to listen, and the music I heard coming out of the speakers confirmed that following my heart to Memphis had absolutely been the right thing to do.

For a year and a half, that one song was the only thing I had to show for the project that would become my next album. "The Pilgrim" was originally a stand-alone song. It then evolved into a concept. From there, I had to go in search of a story. As it turned out, I wrote the last song first and had to work my way back to the beginning.

As I was leaving Memphis in the early morning hours after the session, I thought of what Cowboy Jack Clement once said to me about his time spent at Sun Records as a staff engineer and producer in the 1950s. Cowboy's wisdom was, "The best way to make records in Memphis is to start at sundown and quit when the sun is coming up the next morning." Cowboy's words rang true. I had come here to a touchstone of the past, looking for my way into the future, and I'd found it. I traveled on, believing that everything I was looking for was out there to be found . . . just beyond the blinding light of the rising sun.

WALL-TO-WALL ODYSSEY
(Act One)

After the dust had settled on my trip to Memphis and all the proceedings surrounding the close of Bill Monroe's days on earth, I woke up one morning seemingly living in a new world. I felt different about most everything in my creative life. My heart felt fresh, fearless, and was filled with a new fire. My definition of success had changed entirely, and I somehow sensed, from that day forward, that if I was going to evolve and fulfill all the visions floating around in my head, it was going to be essential to keep creative endeavors out in front of me that know more about me than I know of them.

Another wave of fire that washed over me was a new head-over-heels love of traditional country music. I began to view country music as a cultural offering that deserved to be recognized in the pantheon of the arts alongside theatre, dance, jazz, classical, and opera. More than ever, I saw beauty and felt the raw power contained in the roots of country music. I had been a member of country music aristocracy for many years, raised by some of its most revered masters, but now, more than ever, I was awed by those musical architects who'd set into motion a sound and a language which was a simple, heartfelt reflection of the human condition.

Photography by Jim Arndt

Country music's original themes of love, heartbreak, trains, hoboing, rambling, gambling, cowboying, cheating, drinking, honky-tonking, tragedy, murder, prison, joy, mother, father, farming, hard work, hard times, weariness, death, sin, sorrow, redemption, heaven, hell, and all points in between now seemed more relevant than ever. I once read a review of a Carter Family collection of songs saying, "In the light of perfect beauty, tears are the only answer." That quote summed up my newly inspired musical awakenings. I was stirred to the depths of my soul.

In the midst of these revelations, I sensed something grand hovering above me, and "The Pilgrim" song seemed to be a key element in the overall scheme of things. The song simply would not go away. I could not, however, come up with anything to go with it. I knew the answer was waiting for me out there somewhere. I also knew I couldn't find it by sitting still. So I decided to go have a look around the globe. With "inspiration" and "enlightenment" as the watchwords, I named my personal treasure hunt "The Wall-to-Wall Odyssey (Act One)."

One of my greatest assets is the staggering collection of people in my phone book. I began my renaissance by calling my friends and knocking on the doors of their worlds. I went visiting. I talked, swapped stories, took pictures, played music, wrote songs, and spent quality time with some of the most unique people who've ever walked God's earth. Many of my friends are special, extraordinarily gifted people who've touched countless lives with their songs, books, movies, poems, photographs, paintings, and other assorted creations. They are highly celebrated artists who've made this world a brighter place by their gifts.

Photography by Willie Nelson

Photography by Bill Thorup

Left: John R. Cash and Marty Stuart, Montauk, NY
Above: Johnny Cash, George Jones, and
Marty Stuart, Nashville

Photographs by Marty Stuart

Opposite page, clockwise from top: Don (Juan) Maddox, Salem, Oregon; Don (Juan) Maddox, Salem, Oregon; Cowboy Jack Clement, Nashville; The King of Bluegrass, Jimmy Martin, by his tombstone, Spring Hill Cemetary, Madison, TN; Above, Dolly Parton at the Hooter House, Nashville

Photography by Bill Thorup

Photography by Dan Loftin

Photography by Dan Loftin

Left: Earl Scruggs and Marty Stuart; Above, top: Roebuck (Pops) Staples and Marty Stuart, Vanderbilt University, Nashville; Above, bottom: Vassar Clements, Marty Stuart, and Uncle Josh Graves, Vanderbilt University, Nashville

44

Photography by Marty Stuart

Sister Vestal Goodman at the Happy Goodman home, Brentwood, TN

Marty Stuart Archives

Marty Stuart Archives

Photograph by Johnny Cash

Top: Merle Haggard and Marty Stuart, North Hollywood, CA; Center: Bob Dylan and Marty Stuart, North Hollywood, CA; Bottom: Jerry Lee Lewis and Marty Stuart, The Palomino Club, North Hollywood, CA

Photography by Bill Thorup

Photography by Mike Copelin

Marty Stuart Archives

Marty Stuart Archives

Photography by Adam Smith

Left: Porter Wagoner and Marty Stuart; Above, clockwise from top left: Marty Stuart and Roy Rogers, Apple Valley, CA; Marty Stuart and B.B. King, A&M Studios, Los Angeles, CA; Marty Stuart and Ralph Mooney, Historic RCA Studio B, Nashville, TN; Marty Stuart and the Staple Singers, Los Angeles, CA

Photography by Bill Thorup

Photography by Connie Smith

Clockwise from top left: Marty Stuart and Manuel, Nashville, TN; John Lee Hooker and Marty Stuart, Los Angeles, CA; President Bill Clinton and Marty Stuart, Washington, D.C.

Far right: Tom Petty and Marty Stuart, Sound City Studios, Van Nuys, CA

Photograph, courtesy of The White House

Photography by Kevin Estrada

Marty Stuart Archives

Left: Marty Stuart and Willie Nelson, Nashville, TN
Above: Marty Stuart and Keith Richards, Bradley's Barn Studio Sessions, Nashville, TN

Photography by Marty Stuart

Woody Guthrie's fiddle at the Autry Museum of Western Heritage, Los Angeles, CA

Photography by Ron Keith

Marty Stuart

Red Hot Truck Stop, Meridian, MS

Photographs by Marty Stuart

Clockwise from top left: Elvis at the County Fair, Kissimmee, FL; Show Girls, Highway 61, North Mississippi; The proprietress of the Enchanted Images Beauty Salon, Arlington, MS; gospel singers, unremembered town

Clockwise from top left: St. Peter, The Trainyard Prophet, St. Louis, MO; Sir Cordell Kemp, Defeated Creek, TN; Brother Phillip Holloway, North Alabama

Photographs by Mary Stuart

The Lady Who Loved Tammy Wynette, Michigan; The legendary Tempest Storm, Las Vegas, NV

Backwoods circus performers

Marty Stuart Archives

Photography by Jim Arndt

I felt the need to be in the presence of such wisdom and experience.

Touring with the Rock & Roll Cowboys was a full-time job, although between tours I made numerous side trips, spending time with people who had amazing stories to tell—not only the famous people in my phone book, but the folk heroes of the land as well. People who are legends along the backroads and in the small towns of the nation. Along those blue line roads I encountered preachers, Indians, Wounded Knee, gospel singers, a hobo named Saint Peter, a hillbilly psychic, a lady with a silver tooth who owned a beauty shop called Enchanted Images, rogue circus performers, an Elvis impersonator at a carnival, the legendary burlesque queen Tempest Storm, a waitress named Shirley at the Red Hot Truck Stop in Meridian, Mississippi, and several obscure bluegrass, country, and rock & roll pioneers who paved the way for the likes of me.

Every parade needs a ground zero, a flagpole to return to, or a terminal for takeoffs and landings. My house was such a place for the "Wall-to-Wall Odyssey (Act One)." I purchased a 1920s bungalow on the banks of the Cumberland River at the edge of Nashville. I then had an exceptionally tall privacy fence put up around the place and a massive black iron gate installed to keep people out or me in, whichever seemed most necessary at any given time. I had the house painted a shade of grey that I'd seen and liked on my first visit to Folsom Prison. A friend came to visit after I'd gotten everything up and running. He took a look around the main room and said, "This place is from a different time, several different times." The interior was filled with Navajo rugs, guitars, retired road cases from the touring circuit, folk art, Edward S. Curtis prints, architectural remnants, antiques, rhinestone suits, dust-covered trophies from victories past, and posters from darkened stages of old show houses.

In reality, the place was a portrait of loneliness until Connie Smith walked through the door. I later realized that it was Connie's presence that set the standard for what was to become "The Wall-to-Wall Odyssey (Act One)" two years before it had even begun. I've always respected Connie as one of country music's greatest singers. She is my mother Hilda's all-time favorite. Connie Smith records got a lot of play in our house in Mississippi. In all of my years being in Nashville, I seldom saw Connie, and when I did, it was always in passing. When I came in contact, I approached her in a reverential manner. I always perceived that Connie has been there, seen it all, and somehow emerged with a most loving and compassionate heart.

At a music industry event in the summer of 1994, I found myself face-to-face with Connie Smith. We had a great visit. Our time together was filled with music and meaningful conversation. Not long afterwards, we began to write songs together and fall in love. "Deeper every day," as Connie put it.

I first saw Connie in the summer of 1970, when I was eleven years old and she came to my hometown of Philadelphia, Mississippi to sing at the annual Choctaw Fair. My mother took me and my sister Jennifer to her concert. It was love at first sight. On the way home from the show I told my mother that I was going to marry Connie Smith someday. I did, on July 8, 1997, on a dirt road by a buffalo pasture on the Pine Ridge Indian Reservation in South Dakota. Marrying Connie is, without question, the greatest event of my life.

The night before our wedding, we attended a traditional Lakota ceremony. Holy man Marvin Helper told me at the end of the evening, "If you see an eagle tomorrow, you'll know everything is going to be good." Connie and I did see an eagle on the way to our wedding. Marvin's words still ring true all these years later.

Two hours beyond sunset, after our marriage vows had been spoken, Connie and I went high up on a hill to dance with the wind. Out in the distance, a lightning storm flashed in all directions, making not a sound. It was one of the most beautiful sights I've ever seen. God performed a light show for us that evening that was beyond words. I choose to believe it was a wedding gift of confirmation from the Creator.

Even in the middle of nowhere, there was no doubt in my mind I was at the right place, with the right girl, doing the right thing, following the pillar of fire inside my heart to wherever it might be leading. I felt whole. I knew I had finally made it into the inner courts of the spirit world. It was a beautiful place filled with pure and holy light. Looking down from such a celestial vantage point, I thought of the words from the old hymn, "and the things of earth will grow strangely dim." And they did . . . the cares of the earth drifted up into the clouds. Beneath an ocean of stars, I reached for Connie and held her close. The breeze about us was gentle, and for a moment, time stood still. There were no worries, no troubles, just love, pure love . . . I knew my heart had found a home, and with Connie as my wife, everything I was seeking would now have a perspective and a depth of meaning I'd never known before.

Photography by Saunie Wilson

July 8, 1997

Marvin Helper at home, Red Shirt Table, South Dakota

Photographs by Marty Stuart

Wounded Knee, Pine Ridge, SD

Zona Fills the Pipe, Pine Ridge, SD

Photographs by Mary Stuart

Vegas at Night

Dear Marty,

What a chest of treasures! What precious memories are evoked! I'm just beginning to make a dent in that full table of music. A whole morning of Mr. Monroe, a half a box of Flatt & Scruggs, and CASH – wow! What a gift!

And I do graciously accept your invitation to a back porch pickin and grinnin – ... grinnin. I'm good at that.

Please write a song about Bill's lonesom... what a touching story.

Thanks for Connie; an instant de... She's special – also very huggable ... suffer from hug deprivation. ... she told me you were supp... That w...

-2-

...about the flood? I forgot to ask you ... Connie said it was lapping at your doorst...

...ey, thanks for all the other stuff. The ... great photographs and the story. I'll ... those characters to visual reality with ... nail. I've known all of them except for ... smoking monkey and the one eyed all...

Forgive me, but I keep thinking up ...ngs. Here are 2 made up on the ba... coming home from Plant City.

Slow me down
Get me off the highway
It really isn't my way
And it passes all the by ways
Of the life that I love.

My heart is swimming
in the glow of our meeting
Wondering if you'll think of me tomorrow

My soul was lifted
by the love in your greeting
That sweet hello just wiped away my sorrow.

Ok well! Thanks for BEING.

Tom

Marty

Turns out I have 2 copies of the October '59 of Esquire. What better place for the second copy than in your hands? More I could think of. Here also, is the WWVA Jamboree correspondence.

Tom

12/20/18

Marty What a treat! I'm still swimming in the glow you left in your wake. It is a rare happening, indeed, when one's spiritual kin, boots clicking on the walk way, strolls into one's life in such an unassuming yet powerful way. Whatever the intent of your mission here, you have found a friend in the bargain.

Here is a bunch of stuff you requested to aid you in your bragging. Some of it is from so long ago that I wonder if it was really me doing those things and having those experiences. Let me know if I left anything out that you would like to have.

I'm excited about re-tooling to paint again. I have a back bedroom that will become my painting studio. It's small, but larger than the one in which I first painted Lester and Earl.

I'll be in K.C. from about noon, the 23rd, until Sunday, the 29th. 816/753-7510. Then back home to the drawing board.

Have a great Holiday!

Tommy B.

...the sun never ...on the sunny ... The wild red roses grow. ...been lifted by the love ...welcome me home again. ...s Service article in The ...thing to me and I ...been an "Americana" ... Perhaps I need to get ...doodle better than I write.

Love,

Tom

3/12/97

THOMAS B. ALLEN

"The word 'art' appears twice in the name Marty Stuart. Follow your heart and grow into your name. It shouldn't take more than a lifetime, although it seems you are on your way."

– Thomas B. Allen

The first two records I could call my own were *The Fabulous Johnny Cash* and *Lester Flatt & Earl Scruggs' Greatest Hits*. I was five years old when those records came into my life. After I'd memorized all the songs on these recordings, I asked my mother for more Johnny Cash and Flatt & Scruggs music. She bought me another Flatt & Scruggs record, which was an updated version of Lester and Earl's greatest hits. The cover of the second greatest hits package had a striking navy background, with bold graphics announcing "Flatt & Scruggs." It was beautifully illustrated with images of Lester and Earl smiling, holding their instrument cases, wearing white suits, white hats, and their classic red western gentleman's ties.

Thomas B. Allen was credited on the back of the album as the artist who'd created the cover art. Everything about the cover looked famous. I hung the album on my bedroom wall. As far as I was concerned, it was a museum piece. I consider it to be the beginning of my art collection. I acquired more Flatt & Scruggs records throughout the 1960s, all of which featured visually interesting, highly conceptualized cover art. The signature, Thomas B. Allen appeared on almost all of the illustrations. His signature had an air of distinction. Even at a young age, I sensed Thomas B. Allen must be a man of dignity, the kind of gentleman people would respectfully stand for when he entered a room.

I became friends with Earl and Louise Scruggs in the late 1970s. Earl was retired, though he would occasionally get the urge to play his banjo and would have musical gatherings at his home. It was an honor to be invited. When these sessions were held, the house was filled with the best of the best musicians, writers, and singers. I never grew tired of looking at the photographs and paintings on the wall of the Scruggs home. Thomas B. Allen's original artwork from *Flatt & Scruggs Live at Carnegie Hall, Foggy Mountain Banjo, Songs of the Famous Carter Family*, and *Live at Vanderbilt University* were all on display.

Louise Scruggs served as Flatt & Scruggs's manager. She was a brilliant businesswoman with a keen eye for

Photography by Marty Stuart

imaging and the marketing of her group. Flatt & Scruggs were a Columbia Records act based in Nashville. However, Louise saw to it that the artwork for their ads and album covers was created at the label's global art department in New York City.

Under the culturally minded guidance of Goddard Lieberson, Columbia Records became a powerhouse brand, representing all denominations of music. Classical, country, bluegrass, soundtracks, show tunes, pop, and gospel titles filled music catalogs and record clubs with quality choices for the consumer. Some of Columbia Records' classiest releases of the era emanated from its jazz division. Artists such as Dave Brubeck, Miles Davis, and Thelonious Monk created bold, adventurous music that was fresh and considered the ultimate in cool. Many of those Columbia jazz recordings from that mid-1950s to early 1960s period featured equally adventurous, cutting-edge modern art on the album covers. The imagery complemented the music, made hip statements, and set the label's product apart on record racks around the world.

This artsy approach to marketing music was not lost on Louise Scruggs. Inspired by these forward-thinking jazz covers, she began looking for a broader visual

Right: Thomas B. Allen at home, Sarasota, Florida;
Left: Thomas B. Allen's self-portrait, watercolor

Photography by Marty Stuart

born, Mama worked in the big house and
worked in the fields. The master of that big house set us
free in the spring of 1832, when I was seven years old
and my sister, Lettie, was five.
A PLACE CALLED FREEDOM
by
Scott Russell Sanders
illustrated by Thomas B. Allen
MUSSELMAN'S GROVE
WWVA
CERTIFICATE
Watkins Institute
This is to Certify, That Tommy Burt Allen
has satisfactorily completed Life Drawing
as prescribed in the Art Department of
Watkins Institute
Given at Nashville, Tenn., this 29 day of May 1939
Average Grade
PRINCIPAL
John F. Richardson
TEACHER
Esquire
MARCH, 1961
Special
8-page feature:
MARILYN MONROE
ARTHUR MILLER
JOHN HUSTON and
"The Misfits"
Biggest
show
on earth
G. HUNTINGTON
HARTFORD

presentation beyond the standard photo session fare for Flatt & Scruggs. Louise found her partner in the pages of a 1959 issue of *Esquire* magazine. Thomas B. Allen, who was born and raised in Nashville before heading off to the Art Institute of Chicago, had been commissioned to illustrate a story on the world of country music. One of his renderings was of Lester Flatt & Earl Scruggs. After seeing the *Esquire* piece, Louise contacted Allen and offered her thanks and her compliments on the beauty and originality of his work.

Afterward, a warm relationship developed between the Scruggs family and Thomas B. Allen. For the next decade, along with establishing the inaugural cover for *Sports Illustrated*, creating *Life* magazine covers, creating civil rights murals, fulfilling countless magazine assignments along with his own independent commissions, and designing Mahalia Jackson, Jimmy Rushing, and Johnny Cash album covers for Columbia, Thomas B. Allen created a total of eighteen album covers for Lester Flatt & Earl Scruggs. Those illustrations and paintings are considered to be the first collected works of fine art attributed to the culture of country music.

In the spring of 1996, I called Louise and asked if Thomas B. Allen was still alive. She said, "Yes, he lives in Sarasota, Florida and teaches at the Ringling School of Design." She gave me his number. I called him, introduced myself, and asked if I could come to Florida to meet him. He was kind enough to grant me an appointment. We set a date, and I booked a flight. I had no idea as I was walking up the sidewalk of 830 Indian Beach Road that I was about to shake hands with the gentleman who was to become my lifetime professor of all things artistic. Thomas B. Allen was a fountain of knowledge. He was the personification of the combined worlds of music, visual arts, the written word, photography, live performance, and education. He glittered with brilliance, and it spilled down through his heart into whatever he decided to create.

When I walked through the door of his home, I knew

Top left: Thomas B. Allen and Marty Stuart, Sarasota, FL
Top right: Thomas B. Allen at home, Sarasota, FL

I had stepped off into the deep end of the artistic pool. We spent the afternoon looking through his archives, telling stories, finding common ground in music and art. I saw paintings in various stages of completion; some of which were finished and forgotten but should have been on display in a museum. He showed me sketches and reference photos he'd taken on his trips with Flatt & Scruggs and the Foggy Mountain Boys while he was conceptualizing those now legendary album covers.

There were more sketches and reference photos the world had never seen, including images of Marilyn Monroe and Clark Gable that Thomas B. had taken on the set of *The Misfits* while on assignment for *Esquire* magazine. He showed me contact sheets of photographs he'd taken of Arnold Palmer on a golf course in the early 1960s, watercolor renderings of a rodeo, spring flowers, pictures of Wounded Knee, an oil painting of a fishing trip to Havana, as well as recent illustrations from a series of children's books. I witnessed file after file of awesome, timeless work.

I found in Thomas B. Allen a gracious man, appreciative of my interest in his work, although he seemed slightly perplexed as to why anyone would care about what he had created so long ago. He confessed to me that many of those projects I was so in awe of were routine assignments he'd taken to pay the bills. He did seem to light up when Earl Scruggs's name was mentioned. He showed me a banjo Earl had given him. He then played a Scruggs-style version of the old folk song "John Hardy." I couldn't help but notice that he smiled the entire time.

I finally got around to talking to Thomas B. about the Pilgrim song and telling him of my current wall-to-wall odyssey tour of enlightenment. I shared with him my desire to grow artistically and the longing to explore different avenues of creativity within myself which I sensed but had not yet been able to grasp. Thomas B. Allen's response was, "The word 'art' appears twice in the name Marty Stuart. Follow your heart and grow into your name. It shouldn't take more than a lifetime, although it seems you are on your way."

As I was writing down his word-for-word counsel in my journal, a horn blew. I don't know if it was an automobile, a semi, or a train. I made a comment, "I have never lived in a house where I couldn't hear the trains." I asked Thomas B., "Do you like trains?" He said, "I love trains." We began to expound on what a significant role trains have played in songs, movies, and books throughout our lives. We agreed that trains are romantic, mystical things. Thomas B. commented that a song or an image of a train or train station touched deeper emotions in him than those of airplanes or airports. He said, "My mother took a couple of pictures of President Franklin D. Roosevelt's train as it was coming through our part of town in Nashville and as it was leaving after a presidential visit in 1934. I've always liked those pictures." He then went to a box, found the photographs, and put them in my hand. I said, "Thomas B., these are beautiful. I think the Pilgrim I wrote about in that song is supposed to be on a journey, riding on a train that looks like this one." Thomas B. gave me those photos. Those two pictures unlocked and inspired the foundational layer of the Pilgrim's story. I carried those photographs in my journal for the next three years. When the album was released, I used Helen Allen's image of President Roosevelt's train leaving Nashville on the back cover.

Helen Frances Burt Allen's portraits of President Franklin D. Roosevelt's train, Nashville, TN, October 1934

In that one afternoon spent with Thomas B. Allen, I was gifted a professor, mentor, lifetime friend, muse, compadre, confidant, and the beginning of the Pilgrim's journey. As *The Pilgrim* evolved, Thomas B. Allen became the central figure I'd go to for feedback at every turn. His overview of the story and the music surrounding it proved invaluable. After I had written some of the songs for the project, I asked him to illustrate them so I could see what I was writing about. Those images were also used in the pages of the cover booklet.

Thomas B. and my wife Connie were the two people who lived through *The Pilgrim* with me. God bless the Rock & Roll Cowboys, my crew, my manager, my agent, my staff, and my family. They put up with me, but Connie and Thomas B. became my main counselors, encouragers, and critics for *The Pilgrim*.

As I was saying farewell to Thomas B. Allen that afternoon, I knew I was shaking hands with a friend for the ages, someone whose presence would remain with me for as long as I lived. As I was walking away, I turned around and asked, "Would you mind if I try and find a gallery or museum in Nashville to host a retrospective of your work?" He said, "Do you think anyone would care about such a thing?" I said. "Absolutely!"

Back in Nashville, my first call was to the director of the Country Music Hall of Fame, Kyle Young. He loved the idea; however, the Hall of Fame was in the initial stages of a building campaign, and a new art exhibition wasn't a primary focus at the time. Kyle suggested I contact a lady who is a lifelong crusader for the arts and the head of the Nashville Arts Commission, Anne Brown. I reached out to Anne, told her my Thomas B. Allen story, and she agreed

Thomas B. Allen's reference photos, country show, Jimmy Martin and the Sunny Mountain Boys and Grandpa Jones, Buffalo, NY, 1959 to help me curate a retrospective of his work.

After Anne agreed to sponsor the exhibition, looking for Thomas B. Allen's work became a part of my wall-to-wall odyssey. For the next several months, his paintings seemed to divinely fall out of the sky and into my hands. Many had been lost, forgotten, or hidden away for over a quarter of a century. After I'd acquired several pieces, the walls of my basement became an informal art gallery that served as an "off-Broadway" staging ground for the Thomas B. Allen exhibition.

The project took three years to accomplish, but it happened. The Ryman Auditorium became the setting for the exhibition. A concert featuring me, Earl Scruggs, Janette Carter, Uncle Josh Graves, Connie Smith, Leroy Troy, and Thomas B. and Laura Allen's daughter, Hillary, along with various fiddlers, poets, and square dancers, was organized to kick off the exhibition and celebrate Thomas B. Allen's return to his hometown of Nashville.

Before I cleared my basement and sent Thomas B's works downtown to be displayed at the Ryman, I counted over twenty pieces of art pertaining to Lester Flatt, Earl Scruggs, and the Foggy Mountain Boys. While I was taking inventory that evening, an idea came waltzing through the room. Connie and I agreed that those paintings in our house were all the reasons we needed to invite Thomas B. Allen, his wife Laura, their daughter Hillary, and a hand-picked group of musical icons, friends, and family to our home on the river for a musical gathering and Sunday dinner the weekend before the Ryman festivities were set to take place. On a pretty summer afternoon in June 1997, Connie and I stood at the kitchen window and watched as Lester Flatt's wife, Gladys, and their granddaughter,

Photography by Thomas B. Allen

Photography by Marty Stuart

Photography by Marty Stuart

Clockwise from top left: "Thomas B. Allen: The Journey of an American Illustrator," Ryman Auditorium, Nashville, TN; Thomas B. Allen; pre-show, The Mother Church of Country Music

Opposite page: Foggy Mountain Boys reunion, Sunday gathering at Marty and Connie's house - clockwise from bottom left: Earl Scruggs and Uncle Josh Graves; Everette Lilly, Earl Scruggs, Curly Seckler, and Uncle Josh Graves; Marty Stuart and Earl Scruggs; Marty Stuart, Earl Scruggs, Connie Smith, Hilda Stuart, Louise Scruggs, and Uncle Josh Graves, Melissa Scruggs

Tammy; Earl and Louise Scruggs; and all the living members of the Foggy Mountain Boys and their families walked up our driveway. They came to honor Thomas B. Allen, play music, see each other one last time, love, forgive, and heal.

It was a scene of wonder and beauty—a cherished gathering of musical heroes that turned history into scripture and transformed it into a gallery of art, courtesy of Thomas B. Allen. It was a blessed afternoon that served as the corridor that led to the overture of the overall soundscape of *The Pilgrim.*

Photographs by Thomas B. Allen

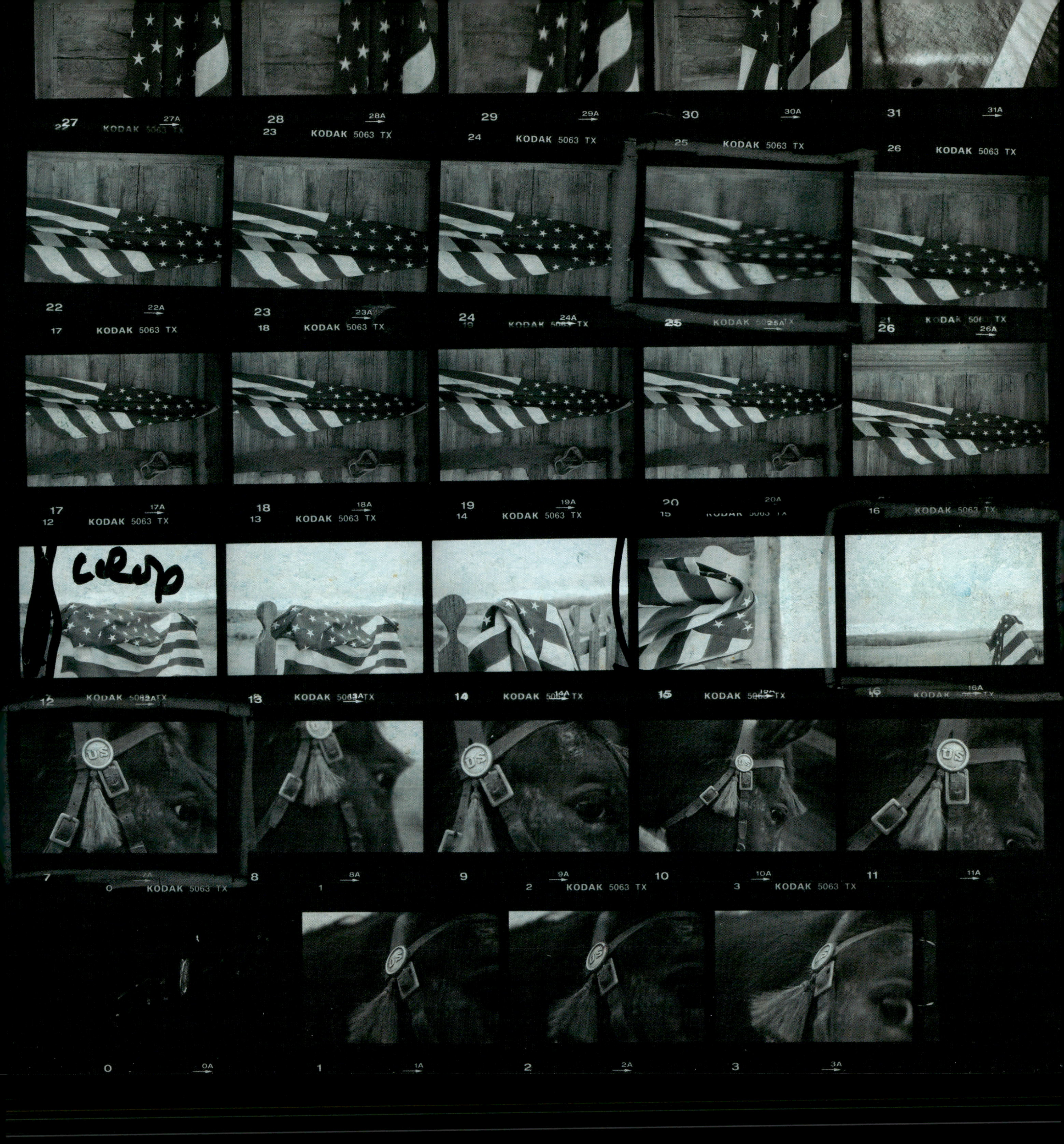
crop
KODAK 5063 TX

EARTHQUAKE
Room 714

"Within the shadows of an O. Winston Link photograph is where my imagination first caught a glimpse of The Pilgrim." – Marty Stuart

There's a saying in Nashville: "It all begins with a song." The avalanche of words and music that became the story of *The Pilgrim*, however, began not with a song but with the inspiration sent forth from those two sepia photographs of President Franklin D. Roosevelt's train given to me by Thomas B. Allen.

Those pictures lived in my writing journal. It must have been a lonely place with plenty of room to spare for those photographs. The only neighbor they had in that book was the song I'd written in Memphis. When I'd take those pictures out and look at them, they seemed to talk to me. They told me stories of trains, train tracks, and train yards. I could hear train horns, the rattle of boxcars, and the banter between engineers, firemen, and brakemen, as well as the echo coming from inside of forgotten train stations filled with phantom travelers en route to the unknown.

A great deal of the power and mystique in the Roosevelt train shots is knowing the president is inside that Pullman, sitting in his wheelchair, nobly abiding his pain while carrying forth the burdens, hopes, and dreams of the American people upon his frail shoulders. The president rides through the world, locked away, untouchable, in this soot-covered bullet.

A powerful technique in theatre is the unseen, the unspoken, or the imagined, leaving the viewer or listener to decide what lies behind the closed door. What makes the Roosevelt train images all the more compelling is the absence of the president himself, as opposed to a scene where he is propped up, in character, dutifully smiling and waving as if everything is glorious.

Another photographer who beautifully captured the mysterious form of trains was O. Winston Link. Mr. Link photographed trains at night. He worked with an elaborately designed system of flash pots, giving his images a ghostly aura. His pictures were filled with riddles without answers. As we follow O. Winston Link into the dark, he thrills with his shadows and the wonder of who's in there, looking out at us.

Within the shadows of an O. Winston Link photograph is where my imagination first caught a glimpse of *The Pilgrim*. He was moving about the trains, wounded, traveling by night, on the run, wide open and gaining speed, yet running out of road at every turn. Whatever he was trying to outrun had him on a suicide mission, although I wondered if he truly wanted to die. At this point, *The Pilgrim* and

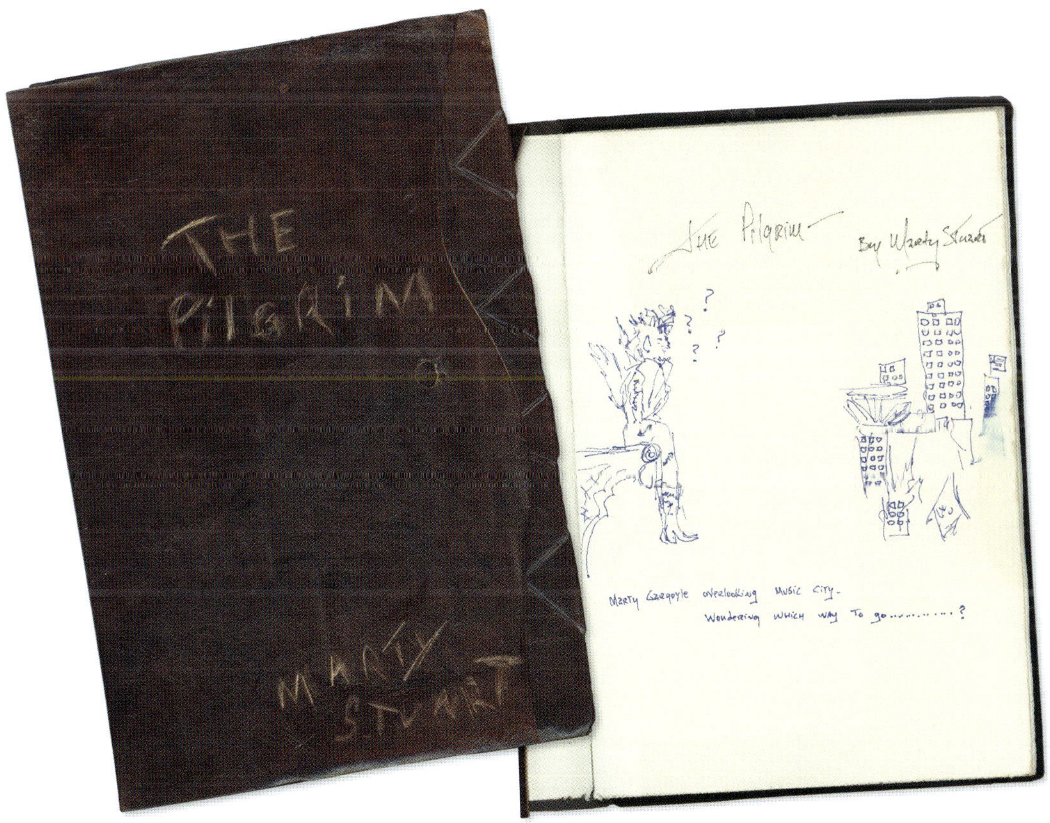

his story were mere fiction. However, the character and his story seemed to be unfolding and moving toward me while patience, being the aggravating mistress she is, sat calmly off to the side and taught me the virtue of grace while waiting in three-quarter time.

Marty Stuart Archives

On one of my wall-to-wall visits to Los Angeles, a tragic story occupied the forefront of the local news. A husband who'd suspected his wife of cheating came home one afternoon, called his wife and children together, and began filling the air with rage. At the peak of his tirade, he pulled a gun and placed it to his head. With his wife and children crying, begging, and pleading, the distraught man mumbled the words, "I can't take this anymore." He then pulled the trigger, taking his own life. This story was being discussed by the group of people with whom I was having dinner one evening.

The sad tale reminded me of a similar tragedy that occurred in my hometown of Philadelphia, Mississippi when I was a kid. I hadn't thought of the incident in years, but as I told the story, the details reappeared. I think perhaps the reason I'd pushed it so far back into my memory was that the man at the center of the tragedy was a friend of our family, and we were deeply saddened by the circumstances. The friend's name was Norman. Norman was always kind to me, but, even as a kid, when I was around him I'd sometimes get the feeling that something inside him was beyond his control. One day he was bound to explode.

Everyone in town was shocked when Rita, the town beauty queen, married cross-eyed Norman. Rita was a hellion, a spitfire of a girl bent on proving to her family, and anyone else who cared to notice, that no one was going to tell her what to do or how to live her life. To emphasize her point, Rita woke up one morning and without warning married Norman "just for the hell of it," as she later admitted. It was a spectacular act of rebellion. The news bordered on the fantastic. Rita's father, upon hearing he had a new son-in-law, said, "Well, she's met her match this time. God help her."

Rita and Norman appeared happy for a short time, then all the inevitable heartaches began to come. Rita found herself living in a house with a madman. Norman dictated what she wore and who she could and couldn't talk to, all the while alienating almost everyone in her family. He was a rage-a-holic, sparked by jealousy, even locking Rita in a closet as punishment for talking to a man for a minute too long at a local store. Rita held a job at the local hospital. After her marriage to Norman, her coworkers couldn't help but notice a drastic change in the girl who had always been full of sass and fire. She now kept mostly to herself, except for time spent with a gentleman coworker, usually in the hospital break room.

The gentleman came from Meridian, a town thirty-five miles away, and knew little of life in our town beyond his job. He fell hard for Rita after meeting her. By his account, it was love at first sight. He proposed marriage to Rita one month after meeting her. Rita enjoyed his company, warming to his affections though never crossing the invisible sacred line of fidelity. And in the course of their conversations, the one thing Rita neglected to tell the man from Meridian was that she was married.

Dead trains, photographs by Marty Stuart

Photographs by Marty Stuart

Back at home, Norman was feeling Rita's chill. He believed she was on the verge of leaving him. He suspected there was another man, although he couldn't prove it. And it drove him mad.

Norman came home one afternoon after work, and once again, Rita wasn't there. He wrote her a letter, put it in the pocket of his coat, got his gun, and went in search of her. He found her sitting in the break room at the hospital, talking and holding hands with her friend. Norman went into a rage and began making threats. He grabbed Rita, held her, told her he loved her, then threatened to kill her. Her friend, not knowing who Norman was, immediately jumped up to defend her.

Rita finally had to confess she was married and asked her friend to step aside. By then, Norman was completely out of his mind. As the room filled with security guards, police officers, and coworkers, Norman dead-eyed Rita's friend, pointed his finger in the man's face, and mumbled, "I just wanted to meet the son of a bitch that tore up my home and to let him see what it's done to me."

Rita's friend tried to reason with Norman, telling him that he did not know she was married and there was no cause for trouble. "I give you my word I will never as much as speak to her again," he promised. "Besides, we have done absolutely nothing wrong."

Norman wouldn't hear it. He kissed Rita and told her he loved her more than life itself. He handed her the letter he'd written, drew his gun, waved it around, smiled, pointed it at his own head, and pulled the trigger.

After Norman's funeral, Rita soon left town to distance herself from the scandal. Her friend stayed on for a while but eventually left as well, fleeing bad memories, small-town gossip, and the horror of Norman's suicide that replayed nightly in his mind.

The most heart-wrenching part of the story is this man truly loved Rita, and Rita found herself falling for him, although she couldn't let it be known. The only thing the man was guilty of was falling in love with a woman he didn't know was married. His way of dealing with the insanity that had overtaken his life was drinking.

He dismissed himself from life. He rid himself of every connotation possible concerning the man in his mirror. He walked away from his job, everyone he knew and loved, and gave away all his earthly possessions. He then began his wilderness journey, hitchhiking from Meridian to Memphis, Tennessee. In his new life as a drunken vagrant, he went to the Memphis train yards, hopped a boxcar, and began his cross-country trip into the unknown. His master plan was to ride the rails and stay drunk until he made it to the cold waters of the Pacific Ocean. The Pacific was the graveyard in which he wanted to die and be entombed, the only place he could think of that was vast enough to contain his heartache.

From Memphis on, the man who was a portrait of pain and loneliness was privy to a series of jails, drunken rain-soaked days crouched beneath underpasses, cold sleepless nights spent in cardboard boxes in dark alleys, hobo camps, and scenes of fights and killings, all underscored with the ambient sounds of trains and the distant toning of Salvation Army bells. He became one of a million in an outsiders' parade of sad faces, an unwelcomed visitor in a string of forgotten towns: towns with troublesome edges, towns where dying is easier than living.

The one thing this troubled soul could not outrun, however, was the ghost of Rita. He loved her, dreamed of her, and cried for her. No amount of liquor could make her disappear from his mind.

One of the tear-stained towns from days gone by where Rita's friend left another piece of his heart was Chico, California. The last time he was inside the city limits was at his mother's funeral, when he was twelve years old. The beginning of a life pattern took form shortly after his mother's service. He ran away from home to escape the pain of what he did not understand. After a lifetime of running, he wanted to go back home and touch the ground that held the one who gave him life. Then he would go to the ocean and surrender that life to end his pain.

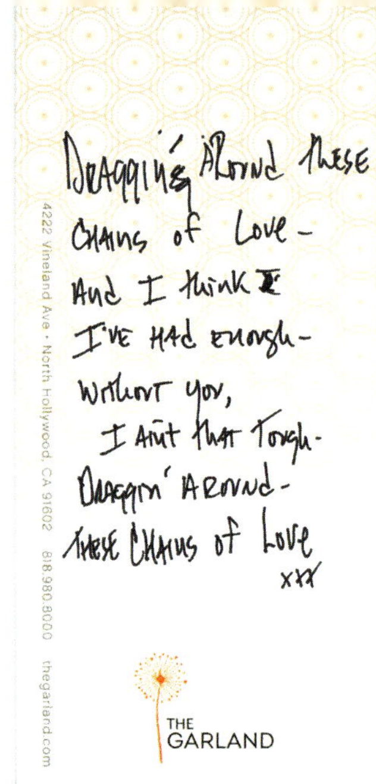

As he later told the story, he arrived unnoticed at the graveyard close to sunset, using the last of the day's light to find his mother's grave. When he found the place where his mother lay resting, he lay down on the ground and went to sleep. He went on to tell that he woke up in the middle of the night with a peaceful feeling in his heart that he had never known, on a ground soaked with tears that he didn't remember crying.

When morning came, even with new-found peace about him, he was still intent on walking into the Pacific Ocean and drowning himself. With his mission accomplished in Chico, he began making his way to the sea. Along the way, wanting to hear the voice of the one he loved a final time, he called Rita back in Mississippi. She answered and filled the line with love and understanding. Rita pleaded with him to turn around and come back to her, so together they could start a new life. Her love overpowered his heartaches.

The man relented and made his way back to the arms of the woman he loved. Soon after, they were married, moved to a parish in Louisiana, started a family, and have since lived a quiet, peaceful life.

The more I heard myself unspool the story, the more it

Photography by Marty Stuart

sounded like a country song in the tradition of "The Long Black Veil." Later that night, as I tossed and turned in the bed of room 714 at the Beverly Garland Hotel in North Hollywood, I retold the story to myself two more times. The tale began to grow beyond the dimensions of a three-minute country song, taking on the countenance of a classical tragedy. The centerpiece of the tragedy was Rita's friend—the man from Meridian who, upon the third telling, emerged from the shadows of the story as *The Pilgrim*.

Fully realized, he was indeed the personification of the elusive form I'd seen lurking in O. Winston Link's photograph. I thought of what Cowboy Jack Clement once said to me, "True-life country songs are filled with drama. There's no doubt that William Shakespeare would have been a huge George Jones fan."

I then began to hear music in my head. The story seemed to invite me to underscore it with the sounds from the overall span of country music, beginning with ancient Appalachian tones, evolving into the tributaries of folk, bluegrass, hard country, honky-tonk, orchestrally framed "countrypolitan," and on into contemporary country music, ending up in some dream-like soundscape somewhere along the outer edge of the new millennium.

In the middle of the night, the entire story of *The Pilgrim*—the ideas for its songs and the music that went with them—came crashing down, literally. I said a prayer that went something like, "Thank you, God, for sending forth this story I have sought for so long. If it's really coming from you, would you please send me a sign? Amen."

I sat up, put my feet on the floor, and started walking toward the table in the room where my briefcase sat. As I walked, the floor began to shake. The alarms went off, and a loud voice came from the speakers in the hallway saying, "We are experiencing an earthquake. Please take necessary precautions." The rumble lasted only a few seconds. The tremor came and went without doing any damage, although it seemed a fitting exclamation point to an eventful night of creativity. All I knew to do was look up and say, "Thank you, got it." I found the closest piece of paper and wrote:

Draggin' around these chains of love
And I think I've had enough
Without you, I ain't that tough
Draggin' around these chains of love

Courtesy of The Beverly Garland Hotel

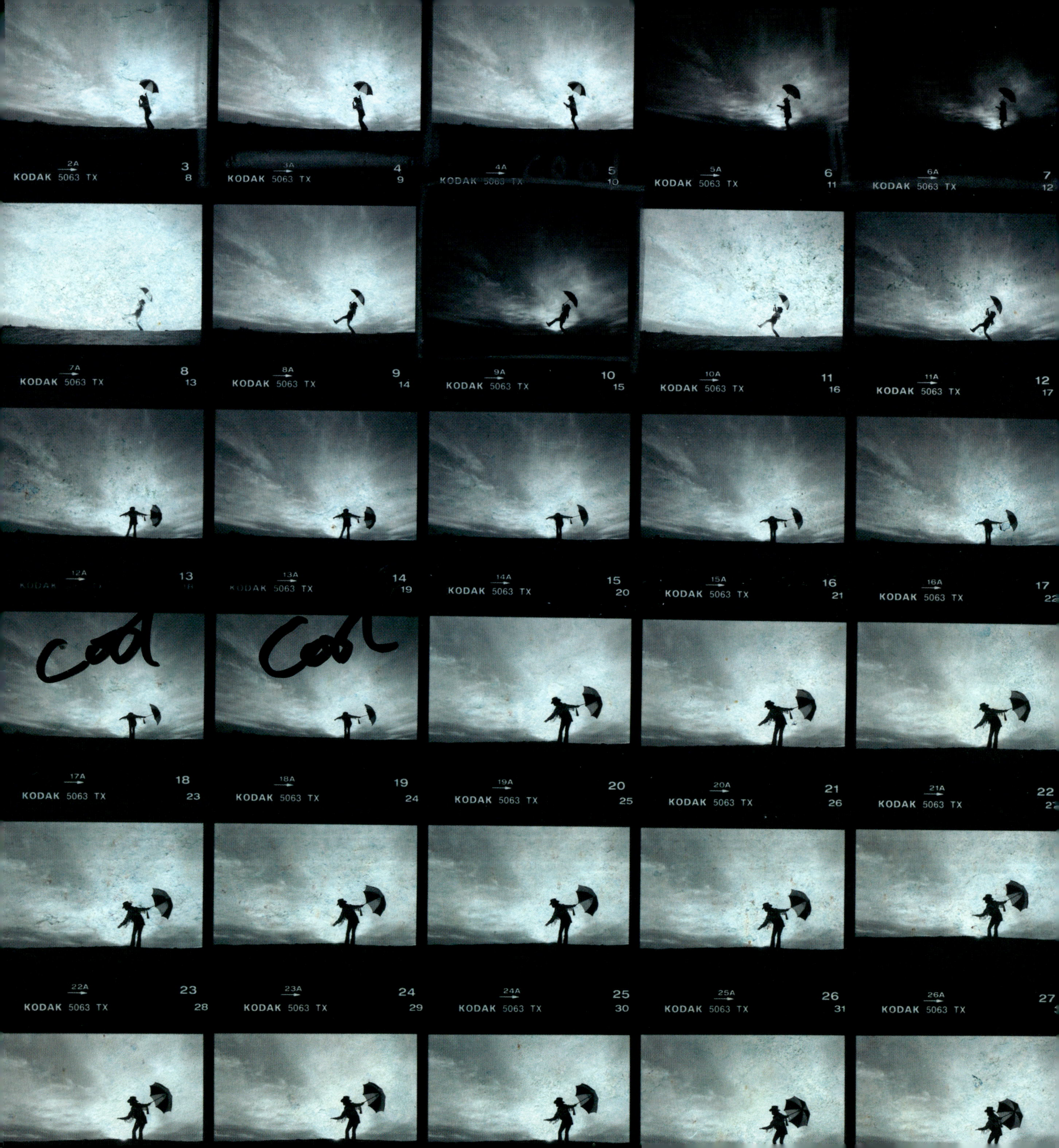
KODAK 5063 TX
Cool
Cool

THE SONGS

Roger Miller had a line, "Good evening, ladies and gentlemen. Relax and enjoy yourselves as we try and entertain you. We have a highly informal show. The higher we get, the more informal it is." When the songs for *The Pilgrim* began to flow, one of my favorite places to write was floating high above the clouds, traveling in airplanes. It became clear that the story of *The Pilgrim* could shoulder the weight of all the classic themes handed down to us by the Father of Country Music, the Singing Brakeman, Jimmie Rodgers. Merle Haggard and I agreed that the subject matter in Jimmie's songs had created the blueprint upon which the overall structure of country music was built. We also agreed Jimmie Rodgers's songs are still among the finest ever written.

The eternal beauty of authentic country music is its ability to meet you heart-to-heart with a nonjudgmental, been-there-done-that understanding of life experiences. Lefty Frizzell's "Long Black Veil," Hank Williams's "Lost Highway," Tammy Wynette's "Apartment Number Nine," Porter Wagoner's "The Cold Hard Facts of Life," Johnny Cash's "The Walls of a Prison," George Jones's "The Door," Connie Smith's "Run Away Little Tears," The Stanley Brothers' "Rank Stranger," and Merle Haggard's "Sing Me Back Home," "Branded Man," and "Mama's Hungry Eyes," along with Woody Guthrie's "Deportee" and Bill Monroe's "A Voice From On High," became my leaning posts as I wrote songs for *The Pilgrim*.

Those songs and the artists who sang them became my invisible committee. When I'd finish a song, I'd ask myself, "Is this song good enough to play for those people, and does this song come within a mile of those classics?" Lofty standards, maybe unrealistic; however, I was shooting for the stars with nothing to lose.

As I traveled, I tried to imagine the world as seen through the eyes of the Pilgrim. He was a stray dog, wary of everybody and everything, running scared, lost, and lonesome. While in Vero Beach, Florida, I heard a train calling from out in the distance. It sounded like Jimmie Rodgers's intro to his song "Waiting for a Train." The summer wind blew, and the words to "Hobo's Prayer" appeared:

Where everything out here ain't what it seems
And when I'm down to nothing, I just go ahead and dream
And face the fact that I'm a circle in a world full of squares
Trading sorrows for tomorrows, now that's the hobo's prayer

The remaining songs for *The Pilgrim* came to me in lonesome sunsets, the wind, on airplanes, on my bus, backstage at rhinestone-studded events where the air was heavy with twang, in a truck stop parking lot, on Route 66, in North Dakota, Hawaii, New York City, Nashville, New Mexico, Los Angeles, and the backwoods of Mississippi. One by one they appeared, new songs with old souls sent forth from a vanquished mythic age, kindred spirits to blue-collar anthems heard on farmers' radios, truck drivers' shortwaves, and jukeboxes in the corners of cinderblock buildings on the dark side of town. I longed for songs that belonged to people who fully understood the lines on

Photography by Bill Thorup

Meridian, Mississippi

Meridian, Mississippi

Photographs by Marty Stuart

Photography by Marty Stuart

Photography by Bill Thorup

Merle Haggard's face, people who regarded Hank Williams Sr. as a loved one, souls who know the full weight of jailhouses, war, second and third chances, redemption, being turned down at the bank, and the heartache that comes with the first night of being alone after losing someone they loved. People who often feel as though they are just in time to be too late. The brand of souls Woody Guthrie termed "hard-hit people." People such as the pilgrim. He experienced hell on earth, all in the name of love. Shakespeare spoke of such pain. In King John, Act II, Scene II:

I will instruct my sorrows to be proud,
for grief is proud and makes his owner stoop

The man known as the Hillbilly Shakespeare, Hank Williams, wrote an eloquently poetic sentiment called "I'm So Lonesome I Could Cry." It's a song which speaks of a lonesome whippoorwill and a silent falling star that lights up the purple sky.

Of a broken heart, I wrote:

Miles and miles of memories
Flow through me like new scarlet wine
And it's sad but it's true, that girl me and you
Had the greatest love of all time

And in sadness I stood
At the dawn of telling fortunes told
With my mind, my body, heart, and soul
Wisdom falters not, it's more than gold
Giving me sweet rest and peace

Thomas B. Allen illustrations, "The Observations of a Crow," "Hobo's Prayer," "Reasons," and "The Pilgrim"

N
R

Pleasure And Pain

1. I give my heart and soul to you
That's all I really know to do
If it's a crying shame, there's just myself to blame
Sometimes the pleasure's worth the pain

2. You cut me deep with that first kiss
Your sweet taste I could not resist
You were too wild to tame –
I loved you just the same –
Sometimes the pleasure's worth the pain

Bridge – And though love burns and burns
I never seem to learn –
I'll walk right back into the flame.
Sometimes the pleasure's worth the pain
Sometimes the pleasure's worth the pain

(Lots of Gtrs)

3 So here I am back at your door
I can't help coming back for more
This love's a hurtin' thang
One that I can't explain –
Sometimes the pleasure's worth the pain (ouch)
Sometimes the pleasure's worth the pain –
(Oh Lordy) Sometimes the pleasure's worth the PAIN

[signature] / Gary Nicholson

The Pilgrim –

① I am a lonesome Pilgrim, far from Home
And what a journey I have known –
I might be tired and weary
But I am strong,
Cause Pilgrims walk, but not alone –

② There's been a hand to guide me
Along the way –
And it's held me up, when I went astray –
And as I stand before that valley wide –
It will lead me to, the other side –

③ At the dawn of telling fortunes told –
Take my mind, my body – my heart and soul.
Wisdom faulters not, it's more than gold
Giving me sweet rest and peace –

④ I am a lonesome Pilgrim, far from Home
And what a journey, I have known –
I might be tired and weary –
But I am strong –
Cause, Pilgrims walk, but not alone –

Pilgrims walk, but not alone –

[signature]

HARIAN COUNTY

WAY down in Harlan County on a Cold And Lonesome Night
A TORMENTED MAN WITH GUN in Hand -
WENT SEARCHING FOR HIS WIFE
WHEN HE FOUND HER IN ANOTHERS ARMS
SHE BEGAN TO SCREAM AND CRY -
AS HE PUT THE GUN TO HIS OWN HEAD -
And SAID its TIME FOR ME TO DIE

HER LOVER BEGGED FORGIVNESS from the Womans Man
I SWEAR TO YOU SHE NEVER WORE A Ring upon Her Hand
Her HUSBAND TOOK A Letter from His CANVAS OVERCOAT
THEN BEFORE their EYES HE TOOK His LIFE
And HERE IS WHAT HE WROTE . . . .

{REASONS}

(1) It was the perfect excuse to get drunk
As if lately I've needed one
It was the perfect excust to
Buy Bulletts for the BARRELL of
My favorite gun -
It was the perfect way to show you
How it felt inside of me
It was the perfect way to find out
How it feels to set me free

(2) I Know that its a crowded
Really this wont TAKE l[illegible]
I'd Like to meet the man w[illegible]
~~I could~~ He can understand
What ~~I~~ He did when he
Broke up our home,
: I'll BE Going now to [illegible]
place I Know ~~is~~ that [illegible]
deep dark And Quie[illegible]
Away from the SHAME a[illegible]
the undieing pain of
me and my unfaithful wife

CHS. REASONS, I keep looking for REASONS
I THOUGHT THAT I HAD Loved YOU.
I did THE BEST I COULD,
REASONS, I keep looking for REASONS
I Lost the REASONS for ME Living -
And that just Aint no Good -

[signature]

Reasons

1/ It was the perfect excuse to get drunk -
As if lately I've needed one -
It was the perfect excuse to buy bullets
For the barrell of my favorite gun.
It was the perfect way - to show you
How it feels inside of me.
And the perfect way to find out
How it feels to set me free. . . .

Chr Reasons, I keep looking for reasons
I thought that I had loved you.
I did the best I could -
Reasons, I keep looking for reasons
I lost the reason for me living -
And ~~that~~ just ain't no good -

2/ I know that there's a crowded room
and really this won't take long -
I wanted to meet the man - help him understand
What he did when he broke up our home -
I'll be going now to a place I know
that's deep - ~~blue~~ dark, and ~~cold~~ quiet
Away from the pain and the undying shame -
of me and my unfaithful wife -

CHS

4-9-97 Weiland Scott

Love Can Go To Hell

I didn't know she was married
that's the part, she forgot to tell
Forget this town, I ain't hanging around
Love can go to Hell

Just as soon as I can leave
I'll be the one that's gone -
Need to wipe it out, to forget about
The futures looking stoned.

[signature]

11·22-98
Hollywood

Red Red Wine, (And Cheating Songs)

(CHS) Red Red wine and Cheating Songs
Lately this Bar room's where I call my Home
Somewhere, Some How my Baby went wrong
Now it's, Red Red wine And Cheating Songs –

(I) For 10 long years not 1 single drop
Now 12 month later I haven't stopped
I'm covering the misery of a Good love grown cold
And losing what's left of my mind and soul, to that

(CHS) Red Red wine and cheating Songs
Lately this Bar room's where I call my Home –
Somewhere, somehow my Baby went wrong –
Now it's Red Red wine and Cheating Songs –

(II) Cigarette smoke, powder and paint –
Can't make up for what is and what ain't
When the truth start to rumble, And it starts to roar,
I ask the bar maid to pour me some more, of that,

(CHS) Red Red wine, And Cheating Songs –
Lately this Bar room's where, I call my Home –
Some where, Some, Some How My Baby went wrong –
Now it's Red Red wine and Cheating Songs –

(Tag) Somewhere, Somehow my Baby went wrong –
Now it's Red Red wine, and Cheating Songs –

Marty Stuart

She said ~~STRANGER~~ TRUCKSTOP where you going —
I see the dust of where you've been —
Seems like the fire of trouble —
Claims you like next of kin
You look as new as tomorrow —
And as old as where you're from.
If I've got it right, and I think I might
I believe that you're a pilgrim —

Anita Carter
or
Emmylou

"New top lines."

At a Hot Stop truck stop
with a dirt floor parking lot
A waitress named Shirley
Poured him a cup of coffee and....

~~For Merle Haggard~~

Call George Jones

TRUCKSTOP

Hobo's Prayer –

Under bridges, Beneath trestles
In the boxcars of dead trains
(1) Living to Beat the ~~cold~~ wrath of the pouring driving Rain
A Silent Society. Moves out in the night
Ragged Rebels, Homeless Hobos, And those like me, who've Lost the Light

(2) St. Peter is A prophet to all the Hobo world
An Expert on everything from Caviar to Girls
I met him west of Memphis on the 8th of July
~~He shook my Hand then offered me this piece of good advice~~
He Handed me A can of Beans – And A Rusty Knife
CHS Then He said, everything out Here Ain't what it Seems
When you're down to nothing ~~there's time to~~ Just go ahead and dream
~~Be proud~~ Face the fact that you're A Circle
In A world ~~filled with~~ full of Squares
Trading Sorrows for Tomorrows, Now that's the Hobo's Prayer

(3) Mother Mary is A lady from down in New Orleans.
She's seen A lot of living since she was 17
She said I'm Bonified, worldly wise with original parts
except for what set me to travelling.
I'm talking about my Heart

(4) She said I can spot A Broken Heart
from A ~~thousand~~ million miles Away –
SOFT Are you passing through. or Have you come to Stay
You're running from A woman, She said with A grin
So what have you got to Say and I said
I AM A Pilgrim ——

Whitey Shafer 5-8-98 – Vero Beach, Fla.

The Observations of a Crow

I. Newspaper Boy Making His Rounds -
Spreading the word, All over town
driving his car just as fast as it will go -
Theres papers in the driveway, papers in the yard
Paper broke a window, he didnt throw it that hard
But it shattered like a dream, down in the valley below

2. Hey Quarter Moon, How was your night
yeah well, any minute now God's gonna hit them brights
So if you stick around dont say that you werent told.
Take it from me, better grab your shades,
if he looks at you, try not to look so afraid -
do the best that you can. But dont think that he wont know

CHS Creosote's dripping - from the high-line poles
Fast as you can count 'em, 12 in a row.
[illegible]ed Accomodations for the so called
OBSERVATIONS OF A CROW.

3 Well that cat down there, hes lovin the flea.
He's married to a waitress by the name of Lora Lee
When they scream and they holler. Man they put on a show
[illegible]'s a protected witness from a Detroit job.
Turned his best friend in, his name is Bob -
I know who got the time, but who do you think got the dough $

4 Take a look at that Pilgrim passing by
Hes looking for love I can see it in his eyes -
Hes running 'round in circles, you can take it from me.
His shadow begs for mercy at every lost and found
In city after city. Town after town
Tortured by the memory of a love he thought was supposed to be

5.  I'm a Genuine Scoopologist, the Name is Crow
Sitting up here watching the show -
In this one horse, drive through, forsaken dried up piece of the world
Well it ain't much but it's my home.
Even had a Queen till that parakeet came along
Fast talking loud squawkin' green feathered snake took my girl

6 Baby's in the Cradle Rocking in the Breeze
Preacher's at the Alter down on his knees -
Praying for comfort, for all of his grief and woe -
The Plate's Been empty, the Choir sings sour -
They need a brand new song filled with power -
A flag waving soul saving tune to make the Church House [illegible]

 7 Little Joey Balooka got a B.B. Gun -
He's Hunting for Trophys, he thinks I'm one -
Look at that Boy he's got it aimed right between [illegible]
I ought to shit on him, from head to toe -
But he ain't gonna hit me, his aiming too [illegible]
Trials and tribulations fuel the Hazardous occupation of a C[illegible]

Vol
Acoustic Pull String -

~~Accordion - Sharyl Crow~~

B. Beckett - B-3 -

Marty (where did this come from / Stuart?)

Going Nowhere Fast

I. There's just too much confusion to get what's really going on
The truth is living out there & it's covered up in stone.
And I get a funny feeling. That's been rolling 'round in me.
I think its time to tell you that it's time for me to leave.
It's been fun, it has been a gas
But it's going nowhere fast

II. Somebody call my number, get me on the phone
Lately I've been talking to myself when I find me all alone
Thinking I should start a fire, burn a bridge back into town
I think that I should go back home, cuz I miss having me around
It's almost real, it could have been a blast
But its going nowhere fast

III. I'm on a roll so I'll keep rolling gaining ground on my comfort
While I need someone to lean on, a tender hand to hold
As I scramble 'cross the beckon call of my own heart's command
I fade and dissapeare into a sea of sinking sand
Like a dark horse running through the past
I'm going nowhere fast

Q. Where did this song come from?
A. New York City

The Greatest Love of All Time

I. I Hear the sound of a train, out in the distance
That takes me back to you -
The only heart I ever met
That was pure as it was true -

II Your kiss is still warm as wild Mtn. Honey -
It lays so sweet on my mind -
It helps me forget the path of regret
of the fool that left you behind -

CHS Miles and miles of memories
Flow through me like new scarlett wine -
It's sad and it's true, Girl me and you -
Had the greatest love of all time.

Marty Stuart - 5-7-98

[signature]
Reprise

Draggin' these Chains of Love

1/ Scared, I've been scared, out ~~there~~ here on my own

out ~~there~~ on my own

Lost I've been lost - (A million ~~miles from~~ home)

Running, I've been running that's all I know to do

Nothing I ~~ever~~ ain't nothing - if I ain't got you

CHS I'm draggin' round these chains of love

And I think I've had enough -

Without you I ain't that tough

Draggin round these chains of love

2. Tired I'm ~~so~~ tired, Tired of ~~losing~~ missing you -

~~Hurt~~ ~~Hurt~~ Lonesome, lonesome lonesome through and through

~~Love it was love, when my heart broke into~~

Hurt - yeah it hurt - when my heart broke into

~~Hope I keep hoping that's all I know to do~~

~~Hope~~ I keep hoping, that's all I know to do

~~Tried I've been tried, but baby I've been true~~

CHS

Jealous -

Worried

Empty

Broken

Restless

dead -

Lonely

Lonesome

troubled

reckless

Marty Stuart

Mike Campbell -

Van Nuys, CA -

11-23-98

Redemption

Sometimes the only thing to do is turn around and find the way back home
When everyway there is to turn has vanished and is gone
I've used up every trick. That I had hidden up my sleeve
I think it's time to reconcile. With what I had to leave

In a little country graveyard in the middle of the night
I'm kneeling by the memory of the one that gave me life
She always knew me better. Than I'll ever know myself
I keep hearing her and Jesus say surrender son and rest

Redemption like the moon tonight, hangs pretty soft and low
And how I've lived up until now. don't matter any more
In the middle of this darkness. I see a light that shin
Like a beacon of forgiveness saying pilgrim all is fine

There's one more journey left for me
That's all that's left to do
And in the dirt He wrote ~~a~~ ~~simple~~ ~~note~~ words that read.
That said "Mama I love You".

G: [illegible signature] 4.24.98.

North Dakota

Like the peace of a dove. — [illegible]

KODAK TX 6043

THE SESSIONS

Marty Stuart and Gary Hogue, Abtrax Studios, Nashville, TN

One of the benefits the country music industry in Nashville experienced during the grand surge of the 1990s was an influx of great musicians coming to town from Texas. Perhaps the very finest of them all was a steel guitar wizard named Gary Hogue.

Hogue was truly a master. When I heard that he was considering moving to Nashville, I called and invited him to come out on the road to play a show with me. Gary accepted the invitation and flew to Oregon to sit in with the band. He joined us at our sound check early in the afternoon, before our concert. Halfway through the first song we played together, I stopped the music and said to him, "You can be in my band, or I'll be in yours. Either way, one of us just got hired."

Gary was a rare find with a staggering musical range. He was a living encyclopedia of country songs. Gary knew the original keys in which the songs were recorded and the specific licks each player contributed to the overall arrangement of the record. His vocabulary and knowledge of the steel guitar were vast. Beyond his own unique sound, Hogue could show you how all the great steel guitar heroes would have played the song had they been called for the session.

Gary Hogue came along at the perfect time as I was writing songs for *The Pilgrim* and making my way back to the classic form of country music. I grew up being looked upon as a whiz kid in a bluegrass environment before going on to see the world as a member of the Man in Black's band. Hogue grew up being revered as a child wonder, a genius of the steel guitar, on the hard country circuit. His world was George Jones, Ray Price, Bob Wills, Hank Thompson, and their likes. Though we were both raised inside the family of country music, the styles of our mentors were miles apart. I wanted to authentically experience the side of the country music world Hogue came from and include those sounds on *The Pilgrim*. Gary became an invaluable collaborator and the perfect tour guide who walked me through the tear-stained, neon-lit, powder-and-paint world of the crying steel guitar.

There was an admirable camaraderie among the Texans stationed in Nashville. They were a cool mafia who camped for a spell on what Hogue referred to as the wrong side of the Red River and rode the wave of Music City money all the way to the bank. One of the entrepreneurs who made his way to town from the Lone Star state was Jerry Abbott. Abbott lived through multiple musical lives in Texas, though he came to Nashville as a song publisher, A&R guru, studio magnate, and stock market aficionado. He opened shop in the fringe neighborhood of Berry Hill. His studio, Abtrax, was located at 2935 Berry Hill Drive. Hogue and Abbott had collaborated on assorted projects and schemes in Texas, so when Hogue hit Nashville, it didn't take long until the two of them were back in business together. Along with being a steel guitar star, Gary Hogue was also a talented record producer. Jerry Abbott gave him an office at Abtrax to use as a place to develop his projects.

The Pilgrim sessions, Abtrax Studio, Nashville, TN

Photography by Jamie Tate

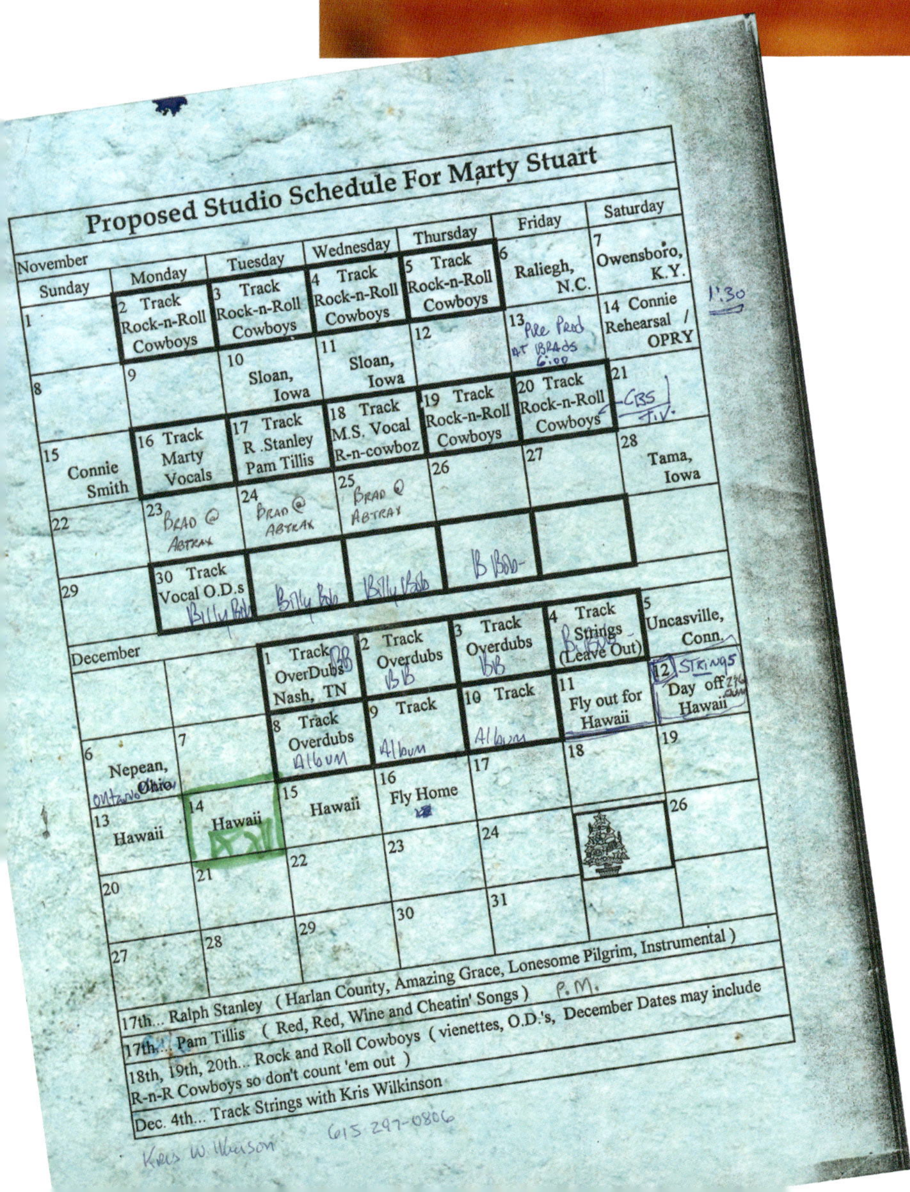

Proposed Studio Schedule For Marty Stuart

Sunday	Monday	Tuesday	Wednesday	Thursday	Friday	Saturday
November						
1	2 Track Rock-n-Roll Cowboys	3 Track Rock-n-Roll Cowboys	4 Track Rock-n-Roll Cowboys	5 Track Rock-n-Roll Cowboys	6 Raliegh, N.C.	7 Owensboro, K.Y.
8	9	10 Sloan, Iowa	11 Sloan, Iowa	12	13	14 Connie Rehearsal / OPRY
15 Connie Smith	16 Track Marty Vocals	17 Track R .Stanley Pam Tillis	18 Track M.S. Vocal R-n-cowboz	19 Track Rock-n-Roll Cowboys	20 Track Rock-n-Roll Cowboys	21
22	23	24	25	26	27	28 Tama, Iowa
29	30 Track Vocal O.D.s					
December						
		1 Track OverDubs Nash, TN	2 Track Overdubs	3 Track Overdubs	4 Track Strings (Leave Out)	5 Uncasville, Conn.
6 Nepean, Ohio	7	8 Track Overdubs	9 Track	10 Track	11 Fly out for Hawaii	12 Day off Hawaii
13 Hawaii	14 Hawaii	15 Hawaii	16 Fly Home	17	18	19
20	21	22	23	24		26
27	28	29	30	31		

17th... Ralph Stanley (Harlan County, Amazing Grace, Lonesome Pilgrim, Instrumental)

17th... Pam Tillis (Red, Red, Wine and Cheatin' Songs) P.M.

18th, 19th, 20th... Rock and Roll Cowboys (vienettes, O.D.'s, December Dates may include R-n-R Cowboys so don't count 'em out)

Dec. 4th... Track Strings with Kris Wilkinson

When the time came to book a studio for *The Pilgrim* sessions, I went around Nashville visiting new rooms I'd heard about and revisited some of the familiar studios in which I'd previously worked. As I studio-shopped, I kept in mind a scene I had drawn in my journal. I envisioned old-world fabrics and folk art on the walls, with candles burning and vintage guitars surrounding the band as we created the record. My MCA projects in the last decade had been recorded at the biggest, best, and most celebrated studios in town. *The Pilgrim*, however, was a highly stylized project coming from a different mindset than the clock-on-the-wall style of records I'd grown accustomed to making. This project had a bohemian flair about it, and it was that vibe I was searching for.

Gary Hogue knew I was studio scouting and recommended I take a look at Abtrax. At his suggestion, I called Jerry Abbott and made an appointment. Gary said he'd meet me and show me through the place. On the day of my appointment, Hogue and I pulled into the parking lot of the studio at the same time. When we got out of our cars, a train was passing in back of the studio, blowing its horn as it went by. Hogue said, "That's one of the special features around here. It works good on ballads, and you said you wanted train sounds on this record." It took less than five minutes to tour Abtrax. There was no green room, formal studio lounge, or comfortable out-of-the-way places to hang out. The decor was minimal, but there was musical freedom in the air: no pressure, reasonable rates, no clock on the wall, and the outstanding feature of a twenty-four-year-old, instantly likable, fireball of an engineer named Jamie Tate. And . . . the trains.

On the way back to my car, I stopped by Abbott's office. On a handshake, I booked studio time to begin work on *The Pilgrim*. As I was walking out of the room, Jerry asked, "So what kind of project is *The Pilgrim*?" I muttered something about a cinematic, noir-style concept record that was part Hitchcock, part Orson Welles, and part John Ford, wrapped in the sounds of multiple forms of country music. Abbott said, "Sounds reasonable. You've come to the right place."

On a cool evening in early November, my road manager, Mike Copelin, along with the stellar crew of Randy Childers, Les Banks, and Matt Spicher, loaded our gear into Abtrax. The team prepared the studio for the downbeat of the next morning's session. Mike Copelin covered the walls of the room in colorful fabrics, stationed a Tiffany-style lamp in the corner of the studio, and arranged a series of candles. Randy Childers lined the walls with a host of mighty guitars he'd brought in from my collection. The room was transformed, taking on the feel of a soundstage on a movie set, the very scene I'd envisioned and drawn in my journal.

At 9:15 a.m., November 2, 1998, I stepped off my tour bus in the parking lot of Abtrax and walked into one of the most magical musical environments I'd ever been a part of. For the next eight weeks, Gregg Stocki, Gary Hogue, Steve Arnold, Brad Davis, and I created music and welcomed George Jones, Emmylou Harris, Ralph Stanley and the Clinch Mountain Boys, Earl Scruggs, Uncle Josh Graves, Pam Tillis, Manuel, Barry Beckett, Carl Marsh, Kristin Wilkinson, John Catchings, Donald Teal, Mike Bubb, David Davidson, Stuart Duncan, Tony Brown, Larry Marrs, Rusty Golden, Dolly Parton, Jim Brown, Johnny Counterfit, Mike Campbell, and Connie Smith to the microphones at our gathering.

Courtesy of the Jamie Tate Archives

Photography by Jamie Tate

Above right, clockwise from top: Tony Brown, Marty Stuart, Jamie Tate, Neil Dorfsman, John Saylor;
Right: console at Abtrax Studio, Nashville, TN

From left: Carl Gorodetzky, Kristin Wilkinson, and Jim Grosjean

From left: Carl Gorodetzky, Dave Davidson, and Kristin Wilkinson

From left: David Angell, Conni Ellisor, and Pam Sixfin

Marty Stuart

Marty Stuart

Gary Hogue, Billy Bob Thornton, and Marty Stuart

Marty Stuart and Tony Brown

Emmylou Harris and Marty Stuart

Brad Davis, Steve Arnold, Gregg Stocki, and Marty Stuart

Sam Moore, Raeanne Rubenstein, Barry Beckett, and Marty Stuart

Photographs by Jamie Tate

120

Connie Smith and Ralph Stanley

Photographs by Marty Stuart

George Jones

Marty Stuart Archives

Dolly Parton, Marty Stuart, and Emmylou Harris

Photography by Marty Stuart

Earl Scruggs

Photography by Marty Stuart

Uncle Josh Graves

Marty Stuart Archives

Marty Stuart and Billy Bob Thornton

Photography by Bill Thorup

Photography by Beth Gwinn

Marty Stuart Archives

Photography by Kevin Estrada

Photography by Jim Arndt

Clockwise, from top left: Connie Smith and Marty Stuart; Marty Stuart, George Jones and Bruce Hinton; Stuart Duncan, Marty Stuart and Larry Marrs; Marty Stuart; Mike Campbell

Photography by Marty Stuart

Photography by Marty Stuart

Top: Pam Tillis
Bottom: Barry Beckett

Photography by Ron Keith

Day by day, *The Pilgrim* took form. It was an exciting experience to be a part of. I basically lived on my bus, which was parked in the parking lot at Abtrax during the entire run of the sessions. Jamie Tate and I would sometimes work past midnight. I'd then go to the bus, sleep, and be back on the floor recording by 10 a.m. It was raining creativity in Berry Hill, Tennessee, and I did not want to miss a drop of it.

The Pilgrim sessions started out as a low-key affair. However, word soon got around that something special was happening at this little studio in Berry Hill, and a parade of celebrities, outside musicians, singers, songwriters, and music industry executives ensued. Abtrax became one of the hottest spots in town.

Marty Stuart Archives

As I looked into that empty room, I saw Gregg Stocki, Brad Davis, Steve Arnold, Gary Hogue, young Jamie Tate, and myself. There we were, fearlessly following our hearts, laughing, playing music, living the dream. I was on the verge of a sentimental moment when I heard a familiar sound . . . the famous noonday special came roaring through, southbound, blaring its horn. Like so many times before, it was a perfectly timed annihilation of a tender moment that wrecked what was intended to be the world's greatest ballad. There's just something about that damned old train.

When the train rolled by, tearing up songs being recorded or heartfelt moments such as the one I was experiencing, it was all right. All was forgiven, because the train is family. It belongs in that room and is a descendant

As I began to write for this book, I became curious about Abtrax. I hadn't been back since the close of *The Pilgrim* era. I could not remember the exact size of the studio. I got a tape measure, drove to Berry Hill, and knocked on the door. The building has been upgraded and beautified. It's no longer a music facility, but the studios are intact. People working on computers have now taken the place of people playing music at 2935 Berry Hill Drive. I asked if I could see the studio. A kind lady led me through a room past some nice-looking, professional people who, I'm quite sure, have never heard a Porter Wagoner record, down some steps, and on into the studio. Once inside, she helped me measure the room. The dimensions are eighteen by twenty feet. Such a small space, yet big enough to hold a trainload of magic.

Marty Stuart Archives

Abtrax Studio, Nashville, TN

Photography by Marty Stuart

of the Pan American that Hank Williams sang about. In the Pan American's glory days, one of the technical engineers at radio station WSM would place a microphone out in the field by the station's tower in order to catch the sound of the train as it barreled through, broadcasting 50,000 watts of its wildcat whistle into outer space. All that business took place approximately eight minutes down the rail from Jerry Abbott's studio.

During the passing of the train that afternoon, the old studio at Abtrax was filled with wonder. Trains, country music, a lone pilgrim, affairs of the heart, the passing of time, sorrow, and redemption: all majestic forms of poetry glowed in their beauty in this space once again that day. It was an honor to come back and look into the eyes of a dream that defined such a moment in time and offered deeper virtue to my creative existence.

SIR GALAHAD

After the recording sessions and the mixing of *The Pilgrim* were completed, the editing and assembling of all the various parts of the project began. I quickly realized that what looks right on paper doesn't always translate into a victory that flows from the speakers. I would listen to the sequence of the record, move songs around, add scenes, and delete scenes. I'd sometimes get close; however, I could not find a graceful way to bring the story to a close. I began to think, "I hope I don't have to go to the same extremes to get out of this project as I did to get into it." It was frustrating, but I chose to view my problem as no more than a creative challenge. That being said, sometimes answers and solutions come from unexpected sources.

I am a devotee of Gothic architecture. When I travel, I visit cathedrals because those Gothic masterpieces speak to my soul. They've been called divinely inspired works of art, and I concur. For years Connie and I have collected architectural remnants and antiques from the Gothic age. We especially keep an eye out for unique pieces of stained glass.

On a stop in Austin, Texas I visited a like-minded couple who'd been going to Europe to buy art and antiques since the early 1950s. I was invited to come and see a warehouse filled with their treasures. The couple was

Photography by Marty Stuart

getting on in years and had decided to let go of almost all their pieces. One of the things in their collection that caught my eye was a nineteenth-century stained glass window featuring a pictorial scene of Sir Galahad. I bought the piece, named it Sir Galahad, and kept it on tour with me for a few days. I eventually found a home for the window back in Nashville in my basement/Thomas B. Allen gallery of art. I was so taken with the imagery and exquisite craftsmanship on the upper part of the glass that I somehow missed the dust-covered words etched at the bottom of the piece. Then early one morning, I walked downstairs when beams of sunlight filled the room. There was a golden light shining directly onto those words I'd not noticed until that moment:

Then move the trees, the copses nod,
wings flutter, voices hover clear.
"O just and faithful knight of God!
Ride on! The prize is near."

So pass I hostel, hall, and grange,
by bridge and ford, by park and pale,
All-arm'd I ride, whate'er betide
Until I find the holy Grail.

I researched those words and found that they were written by nineteenth-century poet Alfred, Lord Tennyson. I read the passage, then reread it. Upon the second reading, I could hear the voice of John R. Cash saying the lines. There it was, the ending to *The Pilgrim*, waiting on me in my basement.

Marty Stuart Archives

Later that morning I called J. R. to ask if he'd be the voice of the poet to close out *The Pilgrim*. I was told he and June were at their home in Jamaica and wouldn't be back in Tennessee for several weeks. My first thought was, "field trip!" If J. R. was agreeable, flying to Montego Bay, Jamaica to record a beloved American folk hero in his natural vacation habitat didn't seem like such a far-fetched idea. One of the things I had in my favor was knowing that after two or three weeks of leisure, J. R. got bored. You can only pop so many coconuts, and then the twitching begins. He probably wasn't bored enough to leave the island, but just enough to entertain any interesting offers that might come along. I called my request into J. R., and he said, "C'mon."

On March 7, 1999, recording engineer Matt Spicher and I flew to Jamaica with suitcases filled with recording gear to record J. R. speaking the words of Alfred, Lord Tennyson. Before leaving Nashville, I'd called one last Pilgrim session to record the music for Sir Galahad. J. R.'s stand-in was a man named Johnny Counterfit, who does a

Marty Stuart, Brian Philips, Johnny Cash, June Carter Cash, and Connie Smith spot-on vocal impersonation of Johnny Cash.

Upon arriving in Jamaica, Matt Spicher and I channeled the spirit of Alan Lomax as we set up our recording equipment in the great room of the Cash home. The place is a 1700s plantation house that was once home to poet Elizabeth Barrett Browning. As with most everything in J. R.'s orbit, the estate is special and historical, providing the perfect backdrop for the likes of him.

John R. Cash had the aura of a revered old president when he walked into the room to listen to what we'd brought for him to do. Matt played "Sir Galahad" for him. He listened closely and said, "Play it again." He then asked, "Who is that talking like me?" I told him the man was an admirer of his who called himself Johnny Counterfit. J. R. replied, "He's pretty good. Now let me show you how it really should go." The minute he began to speak, I was reminded of what a true poet John R. Cash really was. His earliest writings dating back to his boyhood days in Dyess, Arkansas were not songs but poems. His spoken word pieces, such as Edna St. Vincent Millay's "The Ballad of the Harp-Weaver" and his own dramatic version of "The Legend of John Henry's Hammer," were but two poetic offerings he performed regularly in his concerts. He mesmerized audiences with his performances of those and other spoken word numbers.

J. R. spoke new life into Alfred, Lord Tennyson's words in an understated yet powerful way, with the grand finale of the piece being Kristin Wilkinson's string section merging with him on the line "said the lonesome pilgrim far from home." The performance is majestic, giving *The Pilgrim* the perfect finale I'd been looking for.

Time spent with J. R. was always precious because he meant so much to me. The days in Jamaica were no different. I left the island with a knowing satisfaction that the creative mission had been accomplished. I also carried home with me a feeling of sadness. For the first time, I saw the light in my dear friend's eyes beginning to fade. I had to face the fact that J. R. had grown tired and was getting old. I didn't like it one bit, and it hurt to see it.

As it turned out, he would live for 1,653 more days. We had more good times together before he left this earth, with the final visit on September 8, 2003, which was four days before he passed away. It was a cherished afternoon. As I was leaving his office that afternoon, he asked, 'Is there anything in this room you want?" I responded, "Just your love." He said, "You've got it." I said to him, "I have to go to Washington, but before I leave tell me the truth. Is your spirit strong?" He replied, "My spirit is strong." I asked, "Do you have plenty of rope left inside?" He answered, "I've got plenty of rope left." I knew better, but I had to ask. The last words he spoke to me were, "I'll see you when you get home, son."

Photographs by Marty Stuart

Photographs by Marty Stuart

135

Left: Johnny Cash, Montego Bay, Jamaica, March 9, 1999
Above: Johnny Cash recording Sir Galahad, Cinnamon Hill Great House, Montego Bay, Jamaica, March 8, 1999

32A 5063 TX 33 28 KODAK 5063 TX 33A 34 29 KODAK 5063 TX 34A 35 30 KODAK 5063 TX 35A 36 31 KODAK 5063 TX 36A 32 KODAK
27A 5063 TX 28 23 KODAK 5063 TX 28A 29 24 KODAK 5063 TX 29A 30 25 KODAK 5063 TX 30A 31 26 KODAK 5063 TX 31A 32 27 KODAK
22A 063 TX 23 18 KODAK 5063 TX 23A 24 19 KODAK 5063 TX 24A 25 20 KODAK 5063 TX 25A 26 21 KODAK 5063 TX 26A 27 22 KODAK
17A 18 13 KODAK 19 20 KODAK 5063 TX 20A 21 16 KODAK 5063 TX 21A 22 17 KODAK
TX 13 KODAK TX 14 KODAK TX KODAK TX KODAK TX 12 KODAK

LADIES AND GENTLEMEN, *The Pilgrim*

June 15, 1999, was the date set for the release of *The Pilgrim*. The day was circled in red on my calendar. I tried to be optimistic. However, the grim voice of reality seemed to follow me around, whispering, "This is not going to turn out as you hope it will." I could hardly disagree. When I'd listen to the record and get honest with myself, the concept seemed ahead of the curve and out of step with the times. It was pure country music, though the record did not fit into the image of what the country music empire was presenting to the world at that time. Plus there was no feel-good hit for the summer on the album, which ensured its demise.

As June 15th moved closer, I began to be filled with dread. I viewed it as a court date, an appointment with sadness. I remembered a scene in Steve McQueen's film *Tom Horn* where he was about to be executed by way of public hanging. In the movie, McQueen's character was innocent and everybody knew it; however, it was too late. A judgment had been rendered, and the wheels were in motion. Just before Tom Horn was hanged, the sheriff said, "I'm sorry, Tom." Tom Horn replied, "Hold your nerve now. I'm gonna hold mine." He then died in the clutch of a hangman's noose, although he left this world with his dignity and integrity intact.

I began to relate to Tom Horn. I had this burning feeling that I'd be sentenced to obscurity by the authorities at MCA Records and die a commercial death, guilty of the crime of playing authentic country music in the country music capital of the world. Still, I was determined to hold my nerve even as the long black veil was being placed over my eyes.

The hardest part in the creative process is the moment when an artist must hand over their creation to committees of people who know little or nothing of what's been lived through to accomplish what seems so important at the time. It's an age-old dilemma. I followed my doubts and fears into the dustbins of history to align myself with creative souls I could claim as kindred spirits who were successful, yet at some point in their lives either challenged or were challenged by conventional standards of popular culture. People who are now regarded as cultural touchstones, masters of the arts, creators of masterpieces of various denominations, were visionaries who enjoyed commercial success, then fell from grace at the box office, only to reimagine themselves and endure various levels of artistic suffering to achieve the dreams that lived in their hearts. Artists who were dedicated to their work throughout seasons of being lone voices in the wilderness, when hardly anyone noticed or cared, yet they kept plodding along day after day, creating their way back into the light.

One of my all-time favorite artistic gladiators is Michelangelo. I thought of the time Connie and I visited the Vatican in Rome and were in the presence of his inspiring work. History tells of Michelangelo's extraordinary ability in negotiating the clamorous tumble of life while riding the waves of art, commerce, pesky imitators, and the overbearing presence of critics and self-appointed ministers of art. Nonetheless, he triumphed in creating unprecedented expressions of beauty. I especially looked forward to standing beneath his work on the ceiling of the Sistine Chapel.

Before we entered the room I was asked to please refrain from taking pictures. I put my camera away only to find, when the door opened, the scene of a thousand

Photography by Jim Arndt

tourists pointing cameras and cell phones upward toward Michelangelo's storied work and blasting away. My heart sank. All these centuries later and there was not one trace of reverence to be found in this room of holy art. Even Michelangelo, the consummate Renaissance man, is still incurring the irreverent clatter of the outside world in that chapel where even angels must hover in silent wonder. I would love to have played *The Pilgrim* for Michelangelo, especially the reprise from "The Greatest Love of All Time" and "The Pilgrim" song itself. I think those two reels of audio verité would dance nicely with the art in the Sistine Chapel.

Another kindred spirit I admire in the realm of artistic struggle is the great photographer Edward S. Curtis, who saw beauty in the lives of Native Americans. Beginning in the early 1900s, Edward S. Curtis dedicated the majority of the rest of his life to extensively documenting what remained of tribal life of the North American Indians. He referred to his subjects as "The Vanishing Race." Mr. Curtis was a successful commercial photographer with a fashionable studio and an enviable business in Seattle, Washington. Life was normal until he encountered the nation's most royal people. As his passion for documenting Native American life in American caught fire in his heart and unfolded, Edward S. Curtis eventually surrendered his successful commercial portrait studio in exchange for living a nomadic existence, trekking across the country in quest of all things Native American.

His initial images of what critics termed "savage life" that he'd captured on his early excursions were met with awe and wonder by elite patrons of East Coast society. President Theodore Roosevelt became a champion of Mr. Curtis's works. Mogul Jay. P. Morgan became a supporter and underwrote five years of Curtis's endeavors. Over time, however, Edward Curtis's benefactors waned, leaving him facing the predicament of either abandoning what had become his life's work or staking everything he owned to keep his dream alive and moving forward.

He persevered and eventually accomplished his task although, piece by piece, Mr. Curtis lost it all: his business, his wife, his physical and emotional health. Even his reputation as an upright citizen was questioned in some circles of polite society. Edward S. Curtis left this world unaware of the full impact his photographs would have on generations to come. His photographs are now regarded as fine art, and Mr. Curtis is revered as one of the grand masters of early American photography. There's no doubt in my mind that Mr. Curtis would have heard something on *The Pilgrim* to tap his foot to. At the very least, I think he

Photographs by Bill Thorup

On the road, South Carolina

O.K. all of you slumbering Bears!
Winter is over. It's time to come and see me! Fan fair needs you. I miss you, and the Rock and Roll Cowboys want you.
We have a new album, a new show a new video, new clothes, new ideas, new songs, and the same old love in our hearts for you as always.
There is so much going on and you need to be a part of it! We're back with both barrells loaded.
There's been a miracle in our band I want to share with you. People are from all over the world just to see
CNN, TNN, NNN, PNN and M&Ms have all sent camera crews to cover it.
What the fuss is about is Gregg Stocki.
He ate a lobster at a
Steve
Marty
Brad
Gary
THE ROCK & ROLL COWBOYS
photo: Ron Keith
MARTY STUART
the pilgrim
The MP arty arty News
MARTY STUART
the pilgrim
BILLY BOB THORNTON: "THIS RECORD IS PERFECT. I CAN'T QUIT PLAYING IT.........
EMMYLOU HARRIS: "THIS ALBUM PROVES MARTY STUART IS THE KEEPER OF THE HILLBILLY FLAME."
JOHNNY CASH: "THE PILGRIM IS A FABULOUS JOURNEY."
JUNE 1999
MCA Nashville invites and a guest to a ver special evening wit
Marty Stuar
"Marty Stuart has connected w Pilgrim,' the most artistically co rewarding work since Willie Nels opus 'Red Headed Stranger.'"
TUESDAY, AUGUST 3
at
THE TRUBADOUR
9081 Santa Monica Blvd.
West Los Angeles
8:00PM
rsvp to Stacey Studebaker 615/880-7
Marty Stuart PRESENTS
The Pilgrim
BASED ON A TRUE STORY
MARTY STUART the pilgrim
Available June 15th
"This is an amazing album."
Don Was
Join this incredible journey across America with the likes of Ralph Stanley, Emmylou Harris, Mike Campbell, George Jones, Earl Scruggs, Pam Tillis and Johnny Cash; as Marty Stuart offers us this profound and powerful salbum of heartache, love, pain, recklessness and redemption.
'The Pilgrim' is the most country album to come down the tracks in a very long time.
It rocks, It rolls, AND it tells a story.
All Aboard

would have admired the Roosevelt train photograph on the back cover.

I think of Woody Guthrie as a personal hero. Woody is a titanic figure in America's story who wrote many of our most enduring folk songs. Pete Seeger once said to me, "Woody was a traveling correspondent while riding the boxcars, looking to the left and the right, reporting on the human condition." As Woody lived his life and created the template and content for every roving troubadour with a social conscience to follow, he endured violence, was ridiculed for his beliefs, was misjudged, and constantly fought commercial entrapment. Some of the songs on *The Pilgrim* are direct descendants of Woody's style. His writings inspired me to compose such songs as "Hobo's Prayer" and "The Observations of a Crow." He gave all of us songwriters and poets the wink that it's okay to spell words any way we'd like, and if a sentence needs to be five miles long, well, so be it.

Woody had plenty of notoriety in his time. However, he left this world not knowing how many musical children he'd have or how grand an impact his songs would have on the people of planet earth. I'm one of those children, and *The Pilgrim* is a project that could have come from under Woody's hat. Had Woody lived to experience all of the hoopla surrounding his work, it would probably have been more than he would have cared to put up with. His son, Arlo, said it best when accepting a medal on Woody's behalf at his induction into the Rock & Roll Hall of Fame. Arlo's line was, "I don't know where Woody is tonight, but I'm pretty sure he wouldn't be here."

I comforted myself with the inspiration of having the likes of Michelangelo, Edward S. Curtis, and Woody Guthrie as soulmates on the noble quest of artistic freedom and vowed to do my best in dealing with whatever did or did not happen with *The Pilgrim*. My main professor of artistic inspiration, Thomas B. Allen, sensed my jitters and said, "Not all paintings sell when they are first offered. Whether the record sells or not is not what is important. The most important thing you did was follow your heart and create what you believed in. You've enriched yourself by doing so." That kind of philosophy was a bit foreign to me at the time, but I knew Thomas B. Allen was telling me the truth.

In the final days leading up to the release of the record, bits of wisdom seemed to fall out of the sky. As I was driving to a marketing meeting for *The Pilgrim* at the MCA building on Music Row in Nashville, I heard Aretha Franklin being interviewed on the radio. Miss Franklin said, "When I sing, I just close my eyes and hope somebody takes my hand." She went on to say, "I just look for a fair shake when I put out new music." I walked into the marketing meeting with that in mind. I encountered a boardroom filled with people I admired, talented professionals who were good at their jobs, hard-working friends who had helped me achieve some glorious victories down through the years. As a team, our track record was impressive. With *The Pilgrim*, however, I broke character and handed them an oddball, sidewinder of a record that paid no attention to the rules. The record was an outsider to the charade, an Indian in the white man's camp. There was no template for promoting such a project at my record company. *The Pilgrim* simply did not fit into the MCA wheelhouse.

As *The Pilgrim* was set to be released, MCA Records Nashville was drawing a wildly successful decade to a close. When I signed with them in 1989, my label-mates were Lyle Lovett, Steve Earle, Patty Loveless, Vince Gill, Reba McEntire, and George Strait. We were soon to be joined by George Jones, The Mavericks, and Wynonna Judd. MCA was the place to be. Jimmy Bowen was on his way out, making way for Bruce Hinton and Tony Brown to go into motion and lead.

Bruce Hinton was a record industry veteran who led with a light touch, reminiscent of Goddard Lieberson's style of leadership at Columbia Records. He was a gentleman, wise in the ways of corporate life. Bruce ruled from the high road, all the while keeping his hand on the eject button and his eye on the main boardroom where all the golden parachutes were parked.

Tony Brown was a master musician whose deepest roots lay in southern gospel music. From gospel, he went on to play piano with Elvis Presley, then Emmylou Harris. After a successful career as a musician, Tony began to produce records. He had impeccable taste and could sense stardom and the flicker of a new trend from a mile away. Tony and Bruce were a good team whose individual strengths complemented each other. Together they created an ultra-cool vibe in the building and employed a hip staff who were committed to honoring the legacy of the label, all the while creating new stories to build upon for the future of country music.

Most all of the records released at MCA in the 1990s were successful. It was known as an artist-driven label, a place where creativity ruled. However, as the decade wore on, the parent label sold, executives changed chairs, and MCA Nashville joined the overall industry stream of surrendering the very last of its mom-and-pop leanings to grow country music into a blue-chip global commodity made palatable for the masses. The hipper, artsy names slowly began to disappear from the MCA roster, making way for foolproof, mainstream fare.

At the close of the marketing session at MCA that afternoon, it was decided that the honk-tonk shuffle, "Red, Red Wine and Cheatin' Songs," was the only song on *The Pilgrim* that had the slightest amount of radio appeal. It was determined that "Red, Red Wine and Cheatin' Songs" was to be the single. A standard light-hearted performance video was to be made to accompany the record into the marketplace. Promotional ads in alternative papers and magazines would be purchased, and more promotional copies than usual were to be sent to journalists across the nation for their consideration. Beyond that, the unspoken word was, "Let's wait and see if anything happens."

As I said before, the drive home from the meeting was a somber affair. Porter Wagoner's words rang true: "If something is designed to succeed, it usually does. If something is designed to fail, it usually does."

"Red, Red Wine and Cheatin' Songs" was released into a radio stream highlighted by instantly likeable, sugary, hook-laden, well-crafted pop pieces created by Mutt Lange and Shania Twain, George Strait's patented stand-in-one-spot-and-knock-it-across-the-bleachers songs, Tim McGraw's airtight Music Row hits, Brooks & Dunn's boot-scooting sonnets, and Reba McEntire's dramatic numbers, which called for costume changes at the end of the second chorus. And that's just to name an honored few. In the midst of those style of radio hits, the sounds of authentic, from-the-heart steel guitar playing and blood-curdling, ultra-cool Telecasters that twanged unapologetically were virtually nonexistent on the radio dial. “Red, Red Wine and Cheatin’ Songs” didn’t stand a chance.

Townes Van Zandt was famously quoted saying of Nashville, “This ain’t a town for minor keys.” Releasing *The Pilgrim* with a loosely committed administrative plan in the midst of this kind of parade was no less than a suicide mission. One of the footnotes to the pop culture events of 1999 is that the kingdom of Bhutan brought television to its people for the first time. In retrospect, *The Pilgrim* would probably have fared better in Bhutan than on Music Row.

“Red, Red Wine and Cheatin’ Songs” struggled, then finally peaked at number 69 on the Billboard charts. Three things happened on that day: my record died; I fully accepted the cold, hard reality that *The Pilgrim* was doomed; and I made myself a vow never to look at or attach any self-worth to a chart ever again. From that day forward, my heart became my chart. A few days following that decision, I had a vision. I was standing before God with a Billboard chart in my left hand and a scroll with my sales figures in my right hand. I complained to God about my numerical lot in life. God began to laugh uncontrollably. He then hugged my neck and told me to come back when I had something serious to talk about. He said, “Feel free to call me any time.”

Back on earth, the message was loud and clear. Country radio said farewell to me. It had been coming. The last few singles leading up to “Red, Red Wine and Cheatin’ Songs” struggled. The failure of this record drove the nail in the coffin. I accepted that ruling with no hard feelings. I thought of what Elvis Presley said to President Richard Nixon when he went to the White House to meet the President and get himself a drug enforcement agent’s badge. Elvis showed up looking cool in a black crushed velvet outfit with a matching cape. The President looked him up and down and said, “You dress kind of wild.” Elvis replied, “You’ve got your show to run, Mr. President, and I’ve got mine.” That’s the way I felt about losing the support of radio. I had to figure out a new show. A different approach was called for.

I looked into my past for direction into the future. When I

On the road

On the road

Photographs by Bill Tr orup

ROCK and ROLL COWBOY BAND

Photographs by Bil Thorup

was in Lester Flatt's Band, a hit radio song hadn't rolled through that camp since "The Ballad of Jed Clampett" in 1962, but that didn't seem to matter. Lester Flatt and Earl Scruggs were the kind of artists whose music was looked upon as innovative, timeless, important, standard-bearing, and revolutionary regardless of what they offered. They didn't necessarily depend on or need radio. The same applied to Johnny Cash. When I joined his band, J. R. hadn't experienced a radio smash in years. The only time he came close during my stay with his show was when I took Jimmy Webb's song, "The Highwayman," to John and producer Chips Moman during the Willie Nelson–Johnny Cash sessions. After hearing the song, the sessions were scrapped, Waylon Jennings and Kris Kristofferson were called, Jimmy Webb's song was recorded, and The Highwaymen concept was born.

Both the Cash and Flatt bands worked constantly and led their own parades. Both had diplomatic status and traveled in lofty air of their own choosing. The same can be said of Miles Davis, Bill Monroe, Muddy Waters, Willie Nelson, Tony Bennett, Howlin' Wolf, Bob Dylan, Ray Charles, Ella Fitzgerald, Louis Armstrong, and the Grateful Dead: no radio hit, no problem. I began looking for the on-ramp to that way of life. A life lived in the land of echoes, where time stands still and moves forward all in the same breath; a place where the authentic song of the soul is welcomed and celebrated, a place where the bleachers are filled with people who don't care if it's yesterday or tomorrow.

I welcome revelations, new knowledge, and enlightenment, although living through the changes that are needed to make new things come about can sometimes feel like climbing a mountain. The last six months of the twentieth century were a challenge, to say the least. I had obligations to my office staff, my band, my wife, and my family. What I had to work with was a dead record and a cold at the box office Pilgrim tour, but I chose to plow through it. During the proceedings I turned forty-one years old, and every mirror I encountered told me it was time for an intermission. I had been traveling and playing music since I was twelve years old, living fast and treating myself rough. I hadn't been out of the ring in twenty-nine years. I was swinging at shadows. I couldn't make it from the front door to the mailbox without getting lost. I could sense blue lights in my rearview mirror in the not-too-distant future if I didn't slow down.

The truth is, I didn't know how to slow down. Hank Snow's song "Ninety Miles an Hour Down a Dead End Street" as well as my line "I'm a dark horse running through the past, going nowhere fast" seemed to define me. In a sense I became the Pilgrim character; I understood his plight. Same hobo, different misery. Rhinestone suits can only cover up so much. Part of my frustration was I could not outrun the truth of knowing *The Pilgrim* was a solid piece of work, my love letter to country music that contained all the magic needed to move the needle and make a difference. However, my record was owned by a major label that housed a world-wide promotional machine that simply let the project die and fade away into discount racks at record stores and cutout bins at truck stops throughout the country.

The fans who were able to get their hands on a copy took it into their hearts. Critical acclaim for the project was beyond anything I'd ever achieved. Tom Petty told me he bought three copies, and the president of the United

States carried *The Pilgrim* with him aboard Air Force One to listen to on an overseas trip. Merle Haggard told me "That record could give that Pepper record of the Beatles a run for its money." The one and only time I ever laid eyes on Led Zeppelin guitarist Jimmy Page was in the lobby of the Sunset Marquis Hotel in Hollywood. When we met, he reached into his bag and pulled out a copy of *The Pilgrim*. I have always treated praise and criticism with little regard. True life depends on neither, but the kind of approval that was coming at me was being offered by people I respected and who knew quality work. They were not the kind of people who endorsed bullshit.

When a dream crashes and burns, nothing really changes. The sun and the moon still do their thing, stars continue to shine and fall, the world keeps turning, and the divine mystery rolls on. Navigating the debris field of brokenness, disappointment, and heartache becomes the job at hand. It's theater. When an unbridled force of sadness is unleashed upon your hope, joy, faith, and dignity, it has a way of testing your strength of character. As *The Pilgrim* died, I felt trapped in a tunnel of darkness. There seemed to be no light, and for the first time in my life, I raised my hand and asked for help.

As I said earlier, I called upon my old chief, John R. Cash. I knew I could count on him for wisdom, solace, and counsel. Like Michelangelo, Edward S. Curtis, and Woody Guthrie, J. R. was no stranger to the kind of predicament I was in. Every word he prophesied over the situation when I met with him has been fulfilled. There were shades of divinity in each and every syllable of our

Photography by Bill Thorup

conversation. A more irreverent point of view that made me laugh and got me in line with the process of lifting my spirit came from folk music prophet Dave Van Ronk. I read a quote Dave had written concerning all the drama surrounding the demise of the folk music scene in Greenwich Village in New York City in the mid-1960s. Mr. Van Ronk said, "Forty years later, on somber reflection, having fully considered the argument on both sides, I have reached what I believe to be a measured and definitive judgment on the matter. Who cares?" Van Ronk went on to say, "Sometimes you have to forget your principles and just do what's right."

Marty Stuart Archives

What was right amounted to swimming out of the darkness, making attempts to move on toward the light, fulfilling my obligations, and letting go of anything and anybody that contributed to any degree of sadness. I made some radical moves. Suddenly, in a matter of days, years of hard work, the contributions of so many people, and a phenomenal amount of fame seemed to evaporate into thin air. I thought it time to release the band and part ways with my manager. My music publisher thought it time to part ways with me. My songs were considered irrelevant, noncommercial.

As I fully expected, the call came from Bruce Hinton, requesting a lunch meeting with him and Tony Brown. The appointment was made. We met at Merchants Restaurant in downtown Nashville. After a lovely summer salad laced with raspberry vinaigrette and polite conversation, Bruce got down to business. He said, "We're not going to renew your contract with MCA; however, we are willing to leave your name on our roster to save you any embarrassment until you find something else." I said, "You two are the ones who should be embarrassed." Beyond that, I thanked them for ten years' worth of belief. We shook hands and parted ways with no hard feelings. That's just the way the game works. Bruce and Tony aren't bad men, just record men. They're pawns in a game of the bottom line, the same as any of us artists; they just wear different clothes. They did what they had to do.

As the twentieth century began making its final approach, I had one last obligation: a New Year's Eve concert at some God-forsaken casino in the Mississippi Delta. Beyond that, the only plan I had was to take off in the year 2000 and start over. No record deal, no new songs, no band, no publicist, no manager, no prospects, and a portrait of a mess in the mirror. From one perspective, it seemed like the end; from another it felt like the dawn of the days foreshadowing the unveiling of the pathway leading to the authentic song of my soul.

KODAK 5063 TX

REDEMPTION
The Afterglow

Photographs by Jim Arndt

The Rock & Roll Cowboys and our crew celebrated the last night of the twentieth century in a not-so-glamorous fashion playing our songs at an unremembered casino in the Mississippi Delta. Connie and I drove down from Nashville the afternoon of the concert with the idea of playing the show, spending the night, then leisurely making our way back to Tennessee on New Year's Day.

At the end of the evening's proceedings, I said to Connie, "I don't want to spend the night at this place." She agreed. I asked her how she'd feel about us driving on back to Nashville. She said, "I'm fine with that." I did not have it in me to hang around, spend the last night of the twentieth century in a lowercase star suite, and wake up staring into the eyes of a new millennium from the top floor of a casino hotel. We implemented Plan B; said farewell to the band, crew, and assorted friends; and left for Nashville.

I distinctly remember the time being 11:40 p.m. when we pulled out of the venue parking lot. There was a neon glow in my rearview mirror coming from the marquee of the hotel. As the scene faded into the charcoal-colored mist of the delta, in the faintest of light, I glanced into the mirror and said so long to *The Pilgrim* tour, the record, and all of the dreams surrounding the project. I caught one last glimpse of a surreal and fading postcard of four decades of life in a most memorable century. The old world of country music and many of its people faded into the distance as well: Lester Flatt, Roy Acuff, Merle Travis, Stringbean, Ernest Tubb, Hank Snow, Grandpa Jones, Mother Maybelle Carter, Tammy Wynette, Roger Miller, and so many more I loved, the likes of which I'll never see again.

To my friend Marty,

I keep remembering a conversation we had, something you said. Remnants of that conversation echo in my memory. What I remember, that you said and what I thought about what you said seem to run through my consciousness in one stream.

Like Connie says you are an old soul.

As an artist you are trying to dig down deep, throwing out that which comes so easily, because of your skill, your talent, your genius, and, most of all your playfulness.

Most of us are scared to creep around where shadows fall, where the soul lurks for awakening, where genius, forever rejecting the mundane, wrestles, like Jacob with the Angel, pleading to be inspired, again and again.

The ordinary comes easily, step by step, is readily consumed and quickly disappears, leaving a trail of litter in its wake. For time, determines the extraordinary. Like the still, deep note that bears the breath of God.

It seems that Pilgrims travel in endless search, while Prophets speak truth into a void. Yet Pilgrims pave the way for all to follow, as with time the Prophet's word proves wise.

I bought a Pilgrim to give to John Cohen. The man who took my plastic said. "This is the greatest CD of the decade. It broke new ground and returned us to our roots at the same time. We weren't ready for it, but time will surely tell. Look at all that's followed."

In the depths of the wide dark sea, a grain of sand, like the artist tortures the pearl from the oyster. Only the artist chooses to venture into that shadow world again, to risk the safety of the shore, wrestle beauty from the depths, once more; like the addicts that artists are.

We watched the country music awards, a sea of black hats and cotton candy, easily spun and ravenously consumed, like candy with no succor for the soul. Unlike cotton, coaxed from Mother Earth by Human Hand, that sweats while Father Sun teases with a bright, white hot smile, leaving us to wonder why we are all still so hungry when we are so full.

You were chosen to wear the white hat and play the lone true note on Mother Maybell's time-worn lair and with your heart pray. The prayer that both awakens and beckons us home, "May the Circle be unbroken."

My heart aches that you are feeling pain. Yet I look forward to the mystery you will reveal, the beauty you will unfold, the truth you will bring to light when you once again,
"Reap what ye have sewn."

xoxo

Laura

A. Laura B Allen
Late Sunday morning, 7 April, 2002, NYC

Hobo's Prayer -

Under Bridges, Beneath Trestles -
In the Boxcars of dead Trains -
to beat the wrath, and the cold driving Rain -
Society, that moves throughout the night
Rebels, Homeless Hobos, and those like me who lost the light

There is a Prophet to all the Hobo world -
Expert on everything from Caviar to Girls -
met him west of Memphis on the 8th of July -
Shook my hand then he offered me, this piece of advice

said everything out here ain't what it seems
you're down to nothing but hope, there is time just go ahead and dream,
that you're a circle, in a world of squares,
Trading Sorrows for Tomorrows, you that the Hobo's Prayer -

From down in New Orleans
since she was 17 -
original parts
my Heart

Am a Lonesome Pilgrim
what a journey - I have known -
Pilgrims walk but not alone -

valley wide -
lead me to the other side -

telling fortunes told -
my Body my Hat & Soul
not
the sold
Tired & weary
Strong

As we turned onto Highway 61, Connie being Connie said, "Wouldn't it be nice if we could find a church to go to that has a New Year's Eve Watch Night service?" That struck me as a great idea, one with much more dignity than the scene we'd just left. While driving slowly and looking for a church house with its lights on, a conversation came to mind that I'd had with the old bluesman Furry Lewis when I was fourteen years old. We talked backstage at a music festival in Memphis that featured Furry, Lester Flatt and the Nashville Grass, as well as other roots music legends. Mr. Furry watched us play our set. As I was walking off the stage, he called to me, "Come here, boy." I walked over to where he was sitting and said, "Yes sir?" He said, "I seen you up there, you've got it, you do. But you gonna have to make up your mind as to what you're gonna do with it. Are you gonna be on the God line or the devil line? Are you gonna wind up at the white pearly gate or the hot gate? Ain't no in-between, boy. What's it gonna be? You gotta make up your mind!" He scared me half to death. I have no earthly idea why I thought of that talk with Mr. Furry Lewis from so long ago. Perhaps it was being on Highway 61, the most famous of all the blues highways. This is the land of Robert Johnson and the legend of his famous crossroads deal with the devil.

Less than fifty miles down the road is Nesbit, Mississippi, home of Uncle Jerry Lee Lewis. I'd called him earlier in the day to wish him a Happy New Year. He told me he was going to celebrate by watching a Gunsmoke marathon on TV. Uncle J. L. L. has lived with a lifetime of aggravation in his mind concerning playing the devil's music in God's presence. All of a sudden, as these thoughts rolled through my head, I seemed to have been driving through an invisible curtain of struggle and heartache. The Mississippi Delta is such a mysterious place, especially at night. It can get so dark, pitch black. Black on black. It sometimes gets so dark you have to look with the eyes of your soul to see what's really going on. The delta is a big room filled with phantoms, ghosts, the sounds of midnight trains, night birds, echoes from ages past. The ground is soaked in tears, sweat, even blood. Like the streets of Memphis, the delta dirt has seen it all. It knows things that will never be told. The air is thick, oppressive—a theatre of war, filled with music born of hard times, the soundtrack of the battle of darkness and light.

As I drove, from up above, I sensed a cloud of witnesses: sanctioned legions of wise men, women, and angels looking down from the heavenly world,

Photographs by David McClister

sending forth love and light. From below, I sensed a dark, foreboding force pulling downward on my heart and soul, plotting evil, terror, madness. As Bob Dylan once said, "I was being pulled and could feel the weight of the line."

In many ways, the delta transcends all formal knowledge. People with great intellectual minds have done their best to describe it. Scholars teach it. However, the best it's ever been explained is in the key of E, told in simple words, shouted forth and played in twelve-bar stanzas by authentic ministers of the blues, native children, nature's dignitaries of the land: Robert Johnson, Charley Patton, Howlin' Wolf, Muddy Waters, and John Lee Hooker, to name a select few. You need not look any further; it's all there in the grooves of their recordings. Timeless works, beyond trends, majestic music that will never go up in flames or burn out.

Only minutes before midnight, my dreamy spell was broken by the sight of a church with its lights on. I did a U-turn and wheeled into the parking lot of the Commerce Boulevard Christian Church. Connie and I didn't have a clue as to what denomination we would be worshipping with or how much church service might be left to attend, but we were glad to be there. The only thing we knew for certain, we were at a church in the middle of a cotton field. I thought, "This little church standing in the shadow of all those big casinos is reminiscent of the story of David and Goliath. There must be something going on here that is mighty."

The first clue that I was right was when I opened the car door. The music being played inside the church had the walls thumping. It was the same good sound you hear when you pull up and get out at a juke joint or honky-tonk on a Saturday night. The church house was rocking hard. Had I not known better, we could have been on our way into a rock concert. However, I could make out the gospel

Commerce Boulevard Christian Church, Robinsonville, MS

Courtesy of Pastor Hubbard

overtones of the song being sung. Connie and I walked in the front door of this house of worship and found ourselves in the middle of a black country church service attended by maybe forty or fifty people.

I have been to Rolling Stones shows, sung "Uncloudy Day" with the Staple Singers as the earth shook to Pops Staples's tremolo guitar, traveled the world with Johnny Cash, been knighted by Lester Flatt, felt the unbridled horsepower of Bill Monroe's mandolin coming at me while playing "Rawhide" with him, played Jimmie Rodgers's guitar, put a dent in the wee hours of the night in Paris alongside Jerry Lee Lewis while listening to him play the piano and preach, watched Elvis Presley walk out on stage, felt the thunder of multitudes of people cheer for me, sung "Like a Rolling Stone" eye-to-eye with Bob Dylan, met and played for presidents, won a few Grammy awards, played music in the hanging gallows at Folsom Prison, lit the nation's Christmas tree in Washington, D.C., been a part of inducting Merle Haggard into the Country Music Hall of Fame, held Hank Williams's handwritten lyrics of "Your Cheatin' Heart" in my hands, held the boots Patsy Cline was wearing when she lost her life, played music sitting knee-to-knee with Earl Scruggs as the sound of his banjo went all the way to the bottom of my heart, played music with Ray Charles and B.B.

Pastor Evelyn Hubbard and Brother Ed

Photographs by Marty Stuart

Grandpa Elry Johnson's house and farm

King, performed shows with Tony Bennett, sat with Sam C. Phillips in the control room of Sun Studio and listened to Howlin' Wolf's recording of "Smokestack Lighting," played "Mr. Tambourine Man" with Roger McGuinn and Chris Hillman, sung "The Joker" with Steve Miller, sung "D-I-V-O-R-C-E" with Tammy Wynette when I was going through a D-I-V-O-R-C-E, and spent an afternoon playing guitar for George Jones while he sang country songs that were hits for other people to show me how he would have sung them. All big stuff, no doubt, but none of the above comes close to the power I felt emanating from the lady I would come to know and love as Pastor Evelyn Hubbard, the divinely ordered shepherdess of the Commerce Boulevard Christian Church in Robinsonville, Mississippi

As the clock struck twelve on the very downbeat of the new millennium, Pastor Evelyn was sitting at her Hammond B-3 organ playing and singing her song. She was backed by a six-year-old boy named Little Dee on the drums and a small choir of people who were singing their hearts out. Pastor Evelyn's musical gifts are of the same quality as Aretha Franklin, Mahalia Jackson, Mavis Staples, and Sister Rosetta Tharpe. Her sound is part volcano, part freight train, and all sunshine. She's filled with raw emotion and pure love, and she is backed by the ultimate power of heaven. I was stunned by all of this absolute gospel dynamite that was washing over me, too stunned to notice that Connie and I were the only white kids in the room. Pastor Evelyn didn't even flinch, she just waved us in. We sat down, and the love began to flow.

I've been around churches all my life. I was raised in church and have played in countless churches. My first public performance was at church singing a song called "Not My Will," standing next to the piano bench while my momma played for me. But I had never experienced anything of this kind. To begin with, I felt more joy in Pastor Evelyn's service than I'd ever felt in a church house before. After she finished singing her song, Pastor Evelyn had Connie and me stand and introduce ourselves. We were formally welcomed, then treated as if we were family. As the pastor moved from the B-3 organ over to the pulpit to preach, I slowly went out of phase with what was going on in the room. I heard shouting, applause, and lots of banter while cheering on Pastor Evelyn in her remarks, but I felt as if I were a mile above it all. It was similar to being on gas in a dentist's chair.

This was not a conversion experience. I'd made that decision years ago. What was going on that night was more about finally getting to the front door of living out that spiritual commitment. Here I was at the getting-on place to those white pearly gates Mr. Furry spoke of, the God line.

I thought I had a pretty good grip on the Mississippi Delta. Truth is, I didn't have a clue. That evening at the Commerce Church, I realized that I only knew the myths, legends, and stories of the place. I had only experienced its underbelly. I knew it as the land of the last, the lost, and those who often have the least. I was not aware of its holy side. I knew the delta as a likely setting for themes such as Hank Williams's "Lost Highway," Bill Monroe's "Wicked Path of Sin," or his "Old Crossroads":

The old crossroads now is waiting
Which one are you going to take
One leads down to destruction
The other to the pearly gates

Perhaps things would have turned out differently for him if Robert Johnson, with that hellhound on his trail, could have heard Bill Monroe and the Bluegrass Boys sing "The Old Crossroads." From the vantage point of the righteous side of the cotton field and the magnificent cloud of joy on which I was floating inside the Commerce Boulevard Christian Church, following in Robert Johnson's footsteps didn't look very appealing. He should have held out for a better deal, although we'll never know what truly transpired between him and the devil, if anything. But here I was coming around the curve into the new century at 120 miles per hour with a hellhound on my trail. I wanted to take the right road, the holy road. The Native Americans call it the Red Road. Bill Monroe had a song called "The Shining Path" that he and Lester Flatt sang. The two of them sounded as if they were prophets, singing out from the Old Testament. Even as blues-oriented and hellish as the delta legends are, I've always believed the delta land to have Old Testament leanings.

That night, while Pastor Evelyn was preaching, I heard a gentle voice from on high, coming from that ancient, unseen world, speaking into my spirit. It was a voice that spoke to me in the most loving of tones. That voice imparted my marching orders for the rest of my days in just a matter of minutes. Years later my friend Mike Coupe would make a statement that would have fit the occasion: "There is a direct proportion between the size of the vision and the time of preparation." I realized that I'd been preparing since I first began traveling when I was twelve years old, and *The Pilgrim* experience had been the first step in a long journey that now lay before me. It was a journey back home to the buried treasure within myself,

"The Pilgrim," a painting by Laura B. Allen, oil on canvas

back to the authentic self that I'd hidden under a rock back in my early days in Nashville just before I lit out to explore the glitzy side of the world—a world that could only be reached by way of the Lost Highway at so great a cost.

But here it was, this very night, the creator of the old crossroads quietly beckoning me to the getting-on place of that higher caliber of freedom the Mississippi River had suggested back in Memphis at the beginning of this journey. I made the step, crossed the line, and instantly felt an inner peace . . . and I said:

Well I'm one day – one day closer, than I've ever been before
One mile further down this tired and weary road
This old world is full of some trouble, so many heartaches I have known
Like a Pilgrim, I keep on moving, cause this world is not my home

When Pastor Evelyn's service concluded, I knew that Connie and I had met and made a church house full of friends for life, and I had made some personal decisions I had to grow into. In meeting Pastor Evelyn, I had no doubt I had met the brightest light in the state of Mississippi. She is God's hand-picked guardian and keeper of the state's north gate on the sanctified side of Highway 61.

The 280-mile trip back to Nashville was surreal. Connie slept most of the way. As I drove, I tried to process and relive what I'd experienced back in the delta. It was pointless. It was similar to trying to recapture some fantastic dream after waking up. The story never translates. It's usually better to keep it to yourself and just know that it's now a part of you.

As I crossed the Tennessee River, just east of Hickman County, Tennessee, I snapped to. Reality came calling. All of a sudden, I was earthbound again. I remembered the facts, and the facts were that I was beginning a new century with no band, no record deal, no manager, no publicist, and no new songs to speak of. In the wake of all of the changes, I was left with a disheveled office on Music Row for my assistant, Maria-Elena Orbea, and my bookkeeper, Mary Gordon, to work in. I didn't have far to fall to hit bottom. However, I had a new vision, a fresh batch of hope, a direction from above, my family, and Connie's love—all priceless commodities. With that in mind, the words to my song "Redemption" from *The Pilgrim* came to mind:

Sometimes the only thing to do
Is turn around and go back home
When every way there is to turn, has vanished and is gone
I've used up every trick I had hidden up my sleeve
Think it's time I reconcile with what I had to leave

In the early days of the year 2000, I did go home, back to my Grandpa Elry Johnson's farm in Arlington, Mississippi. I stayed for a while, trying to untangle my mind and get restarted. I searched for peace and direction for the days ahead. From there, I started over, and all roads to the future stemmed from those days spent among family, friends, and loved ones in my homeland. For a time, I dwelled under the canopy of the eternal trees and survived.

Looking back on twenty years ago, making *The Pilgrim* was unquestionably the right thing to have done. It was the first in a long line of creative endeavors that have resulted in the most rewarding years of my life. The impartation sent forth at the Commerce Church service, January 1, 2000, was to love, protect, defend, promote, and further the culture of traditional country music and its people, and to aid and participate in any way possible in the organization, promotion, recasting, and furtherance of the state of Mississippi's creative legacy. Worthy missions to be a part of, missions that know much more about me than I do of them. As the song says:

There's been a hand to guide me along
  the way
And it's held me up when I went astray
as I stand before the valley wide
It will lead me to the other side

I am a lonesome pilgrim far from home
What a journey I have known
I may be tired and weary but I am strong
Pilgrims walk, but not alone

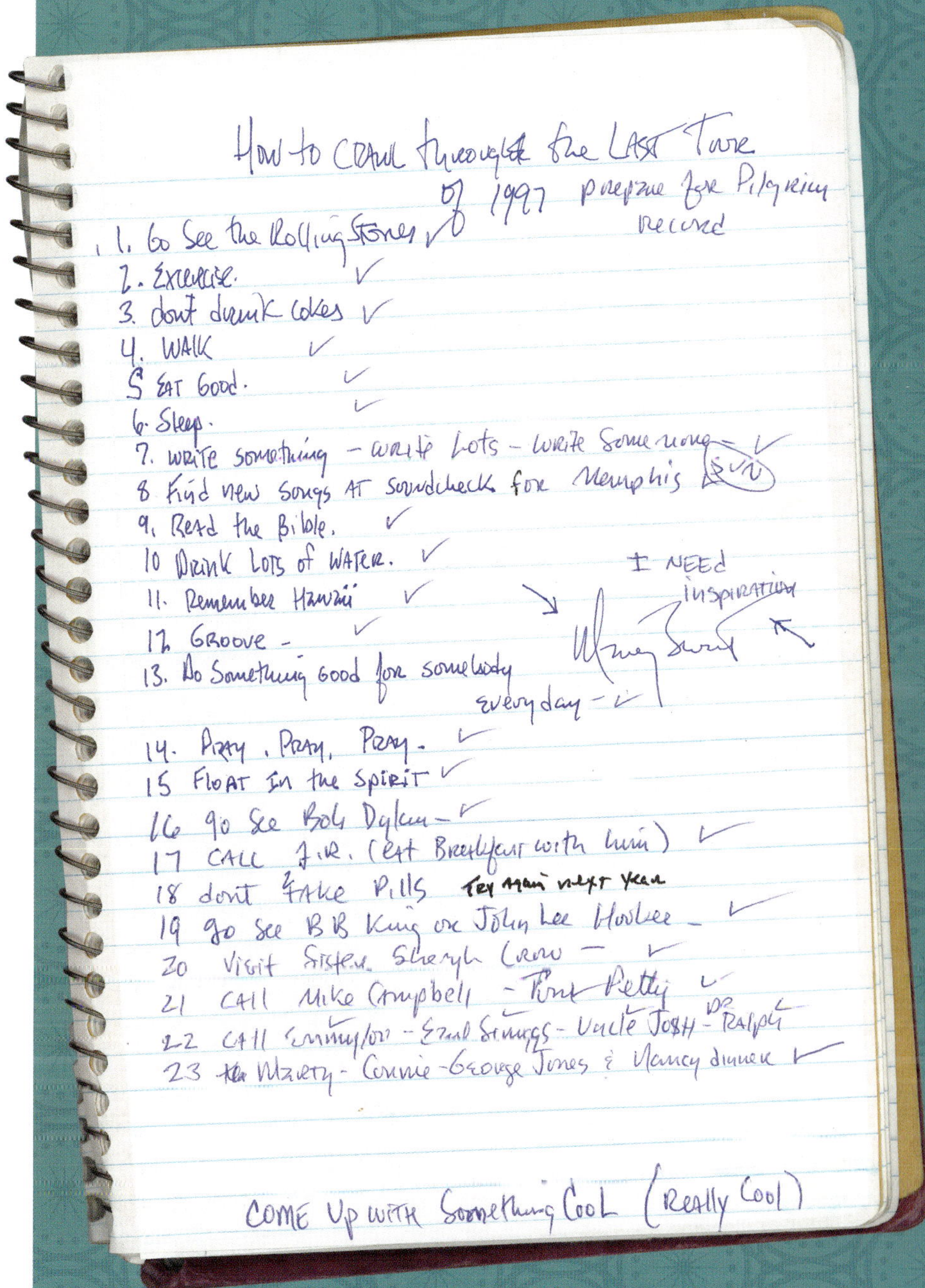

"THE PILGRAM"
LT. VERSION
(NO "GOODBYE TENNESSEE"
OR "IF IT TURNS OUT...")
12/24/98
maxell®
Program No.
MARTY STUART – SUN STUD
Recording Date
Aug 22-23, 1996
Broadcast Date
19cmps(7½ips)
9.5cmps(3¾ips)
4.75cmps(1⅞ips)
Monophonic
Tracks
Stereophonic
2 Tracks
Recorder:
Name
Model
8/22
1. I'm Coming Home
2. Endless Sleep 1 + 2 (use second take)
8/23
1. The Pilgrim
"THE PILGRAM"
ALTERNATE ALBUM VERSION
"GOODBYE TENNESSEE" +
"IT'D BE ALRIGHT WITH ME" REMOVED
FADES, EDITS, LEVELS TWEEKED
12/24/98
6. Lonesome
7. Harlan County
8. Cluck Old Hen
9. Dobro Madness
EARL SCRUGGS
10. Cannonball Blues
11. Cannonball Blues
12. Fiddle & Banjo
13. Tennessee Wagoner
14. ?
15. ? (Take 2)
16. ? (Edit Pieces)
17. John Henry (Full Band)
18. John Henry (Mand/Banjo)
19. John Henry (Mand/Banjo) (Take 2)
Produced By Marty Stuart
Engineered by Jamie Tate
Abtrax Recording
(615) 297-3723
29. Starlight
30. Dobro Story
31. Dobro Licks
32. Colorado Turnaround
33. Evalene
Lot No.

INSTRUMENTS PLAYED ON

The Pilgrim

Don

Mid-1960s silver sparkle Fender Telecaster originally played by Don Rich with Buck Owens and the Buckaroos on "Love's Gonna Live Here," "Tiger by the Tail," "Act Naturally," "Sam's Place."

Used on "That'll Be All Right With Me."

J.R.

1957 customized J200 Gibson—originally belonging to Johnny Cash. Played on "Pickin' Time," "Five Feet High and Rising," "Don't Take Your Guns to Town," "I Still Miss Someone."

Used on "Redemption," "Reasons," "Draggin' Around These Chains of Love."

Guitars on loan courtesy of Margie Perkins

Luther 1

1955 Fender Esquire originally belonging to Luther Perkins and played on the original Cash Sun Records recordings.

Used by Mike Campbell on "Draggin' Around These Chains of Love," "Sometimes the Pleasure's Worth the Pain."

Luther 2

Luther Perkins's mid-1960s Fender Esquire—played by Luther on the Folsom Prison event recorded in January 1968.

Used on "Sometimes the Pleasure's Worth the Pain."

Jamie Tate's photographs of the guitars used on *The Pilgrim* sessions

Ronson

1952 Fender Esquire once owned by Mick Ronson

Used on "Going Nowhere Fast"

Clarence

1954 Fender Telecaster w/original B-string bender originally belonging to Clarence White.

Used on "Sometimes the Pleasure's Worth the Pain," "Red, Red Wine & Cheatin' Songs"

Wayne

1962 Fender Jazzmaster orginally belonging to Wayne Moss. Played on "Pretty Woman," "Only Daddy That'll Walk the Line," "Almost Persuaded."

Used on "Goin' Nowhere Fast"

Buddy

1972 F-5 mandolin copy made by Chris Warner, purchased from Roland White in 1972.

Used on "Greatest Love of All Time (reprise)," "Shout Little Lulie"

Maybelle

1967 Fender Kingman acoustic made for Mother Maybelle Carter. Used by the Carter Family at the recording of Johnny Cash at San Quentin, February 1969.

Used on "Greatest Love of all Time," "Goin' Nowhere Fast."

Hank

1939 Martin D-45 originally belonging to Hank Williams, Hank Williams Jr., and Johnny Cash.

Used on "Sir Galahad," "Harlan County," "Greatest Love of all Time," "Evelina," "Been Lonely Too Long."

Lester

1950 Martin D-28 originally belonging to Lester Flatt. Used on the majority of all recordings and televised appearances by Lester Flatt, Earl Scruggs and the Foggy Mountain Boys from 1954–1969.

Used on "Truckstop," "Goin' Nowhere Fast."

Lucky

1956 Gretsch 6120 guitar.

Used on "Goin' Nowhere Fast," "Blue, Blue Town," "The Vanishing," "Been Lonely Too Long."

Marty

1996 Martin Marty Stuart Signature Acoustic HD40MS (factory prototype).

Used on "Hobo's Prayer."

Uncle Pen

1950 D-28 Martin. Played on the original Bill Monroe recording of "Uncle Pen." It now has a Gene Parsons B-bender and a stack of Fender twin amplifiers attached to it, as well as death threats on Marty's life from hardcore bluegrass fans.

Used on "The Observations of a Crow."

Lloyd

1924 F-5 Lloyd Loar Gibson mandolin.

Used on "The Pilgrim," "Greatest Love of All Time," "Mr. John Henry, Steel Drivin' Man"

EPILOGUE

As I walk'd through the wilderness of this world, and I laid down in that place to sleep; and as I slept, I dreamed a Dream.

– John Bunyan, *The Pilgrim's Progress*

The dream experienced by the protagonist of *The Pilgrim's Progress* became one of the most renowned examples in the seventeenth century of how art emerges from the unconscious mind. Whether or not the premise for the book came to the author John Bunyan in a dream is irrelevant. The arc of his novel resonates because we all have had a dream that becomes intelligible upon our awaking, literally or metaphorically. A good story is carried along by internal tension that both hides and reveals the full potential of the implicit message.

Sometimes we interpret a dream as prescient. Psychoanalytic writing codified how desires or wishful thinking are manifested in dreams through substitution, fragmentation, and displacement. Interpreting the ambiguity of our dreams takes us on an intriguing pilgrimage. Visual artists, writers, composers, songwriters, and storytellers often weave intricate narratives that are incomprehensible at first and appreciated only later.

Creativity that rises to the level of art possesses a complexity that endures across time. We can outgrow something that was at one time completely captivating. We mature. For example, the love of a purple dinosaur named Barney gives way to the study of vertebrate paleontology. The art of the Italian Renaissance spoke in the vernacular of the fourteenth and fifteenth centuries to members of the emerging merchant class, providing ethical and spiritual guidance to the laity. The beauty and transformative power of those images continues to resonate viscerally for us today, despite the distance of time, place, and purpose.

The inverse can also be true. An artist may narrate the episodes of a journey but also be a prophet. She or he can create in a style or include a message that is nuanced in ways we are not ready to receive. As we as individuals or as a society catch up, the art can be measured in the context of a new season. Fashion goes in and out of favor. Art, on the other hand, persists because it taps into a deeper well of thought and inspiration. The artist cannot be deterred. Marty Stuart gave us *The Pilgrim* for the ages, not on a whim. The rerelease of this groundbreaking work gives us a second chance to appreciate what has been there from the beginning.

– Susan H. Edwards ©
Director, Frist Art Museum, Nashville, TN

My girl Nathalie had a very close old friend, Marty Stuart, who was coming to Santa Fe on an adventure. Marty asked me along to make images for his new project, *The Pilgrim*. We went north of town to a wilderness area, to walk in the high desert. Marty, in a top hat and long cape, initially seemed out of place. But this was Marty, the Pilgrim.

It was unspoken, but Marty was on a pilgrimage to a new beginning.

Meeting him brought a very down-to-earth feeling, a connection like old brothers getting together. We knew each other without knowing each other.

Marty knew what he wanted the images to look like. He is a photographer, an image maker, and a visual artist, as well as a songwriter and musician. He didn't want the images to be shot like other album photos, but instead he wanted them to be more about a feeling, an emotion.

I was an observer, looking on editorially.

Two people on a journey – Marty and the eye of the camera.

It was a time filled with emotion for me. My father had passed away a couple days before, so he was on a pilgrimage to Heaven. I was on a pilgrimage now on my own.

Marty was on his pilgrimage with *The Pilgrim*, his new beginning….

– Jim Arndt, 2019

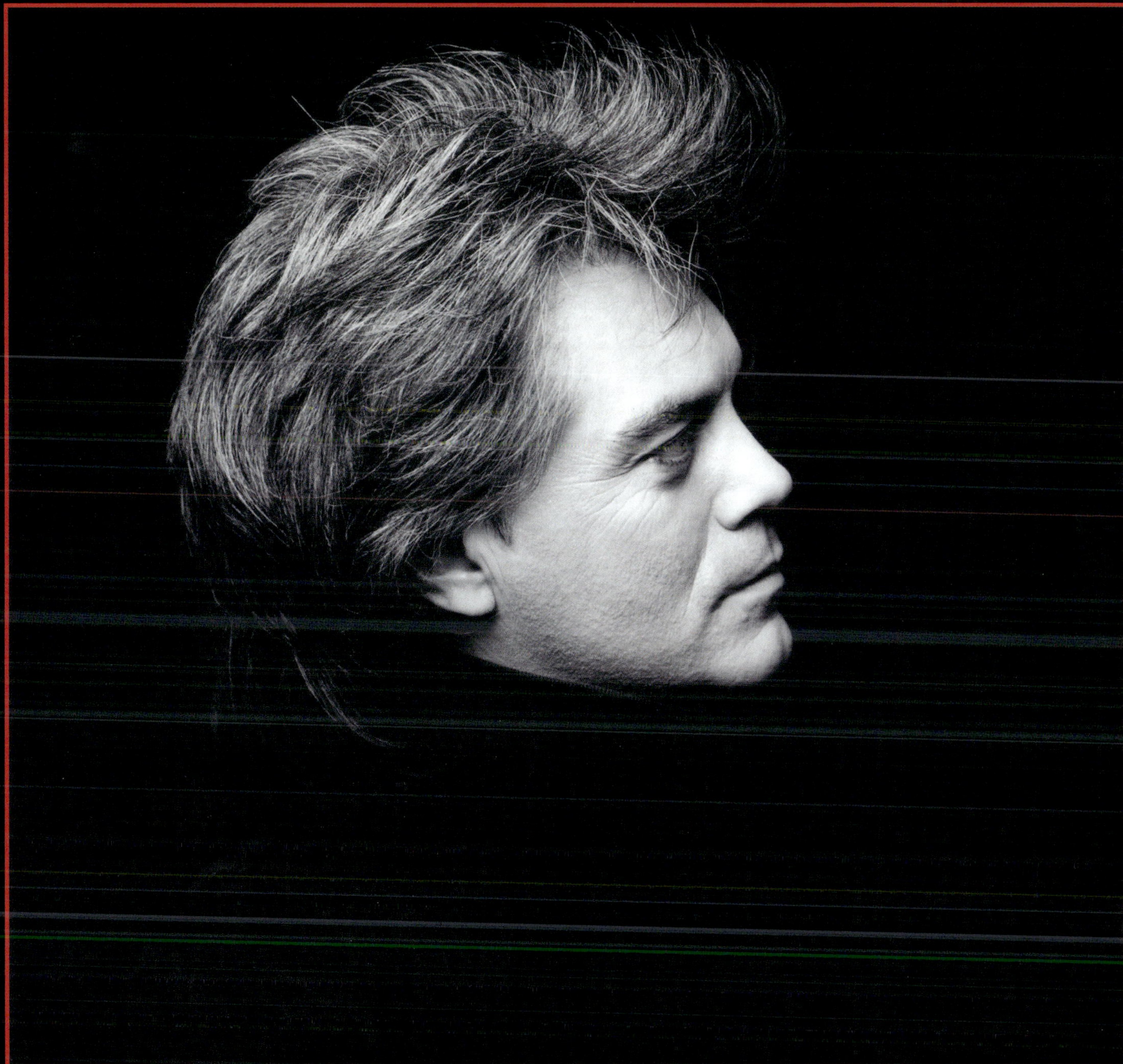

Photography by Jim Arndt

Photography by David McClister

Dream big. Follow your heart at any cost. The scarier, the better. It will always lead you to the right place.

Violin 1

Marty Stuart

Pilgrim

strings arranged by Kris Wilkinson

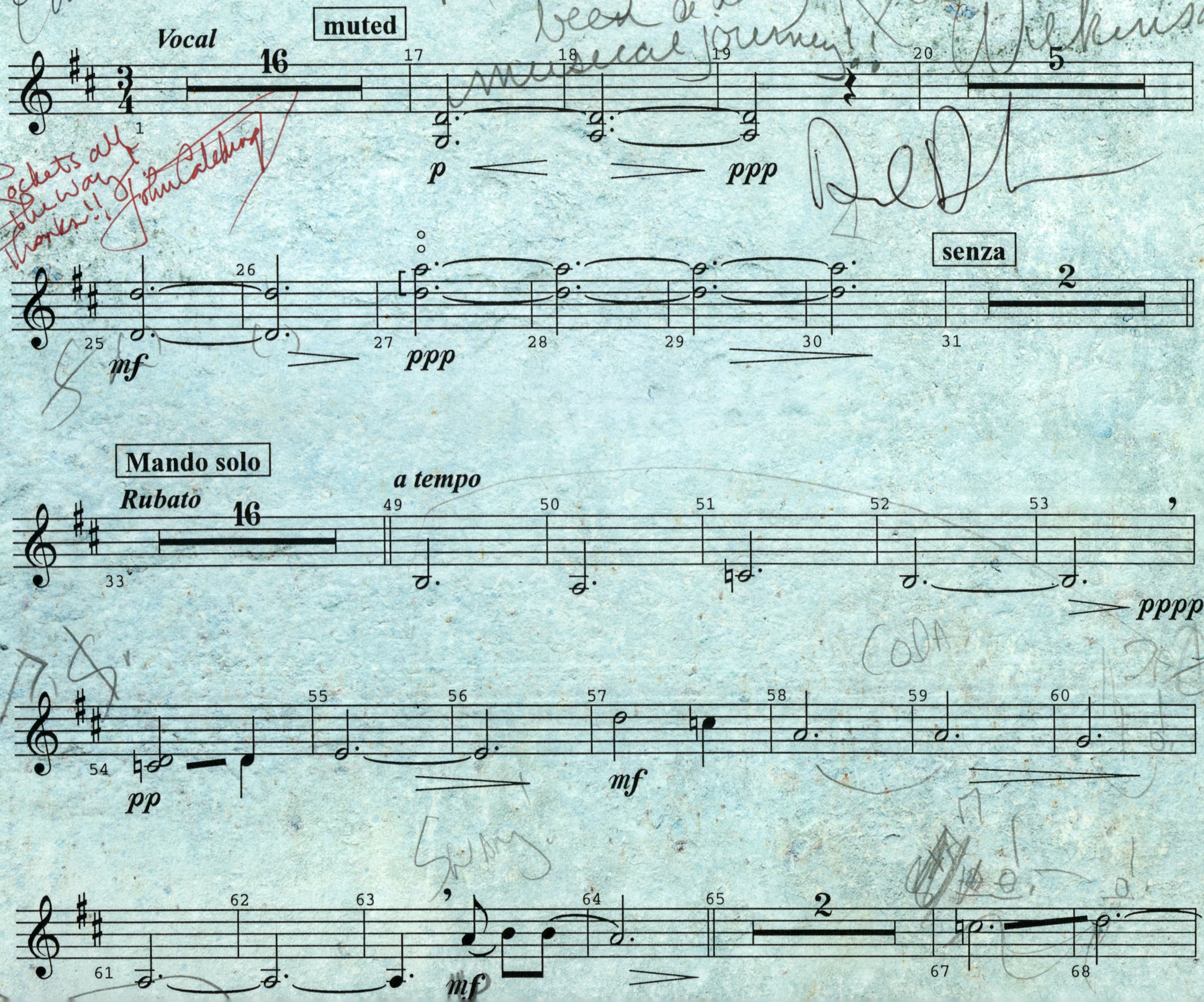

CREDITS

The Pilgrim

Produced by: Marty Stuart / Executive Producer: Tony Brown

RECORDED AT: Abtrax Recording on the Otari RADAR hard disk: Jamie Tate - engineer; Matt Spicher - 2nd engineer / Strings recorded at Quad Studio: Jamie Tate - engineer; David Streit - 2nd engineer / Vocal overdubs recorded at MCA Music: Rocky Schnaars - engineer; King Williams - additional engineer / Compiled by Dale Loyd on a SADiE portable editor

MIXED AT: Abtrax Recording: Jamie Tate - engineer / Masterfonics: Neil Dorfsman, engineer on songs 7, 10, 13, 14, 17, 19 / John Saylor – 2nd engineer; Gary Hogue – assistant

MASTERED AT MasterMix: Hank Williams - engineer

MUSICIANS: Marty Stuart - vocals, acoustic guitar, electric guitar, mandolin / Rock & Roll Cowboys: Steve Arnold - bass; Gary Hogue - steel; Brad Davis - vocals, electric guitar, acoustic guitar; Gregg Stocki - drums, timpani, percussion

GUEST MUSICIANS: Mike Campbell - 12 string acoustic guitar, electric guitar; Tony Brown - piano; Barry Beckett - B3 organ; Stuart Duncan - fiddle; Earl Scruggs - acoustic guitar, banjo; Uncle Josh Graves - dobro; Carl Marsh - sound fx, calliope, organ; Rusty Golden - piano; Mike Bub - upright bass; Jim Brown - B3 organ, piano; Ralph Stanley and the Clinch Mountain Boys: Ralph Stanley - vocals, banjo; Jack Cooke - vocals, acoustic bass; James Shelton - acoustic guitar; Steve Sparkman - banjo; James Price - vocals, fiddle

STRINGS ARRANGED BY: Kristin Wilkinson / Kristin Wilkinson - viola; David Davidson - violin; John Catchings - cello; Chris Teal - violin

VOICES: Johnny Cash; George Jones; Emmylou Harris; Pam Tillis; Larry Marrs; Johnny Counterfeit; Brad Davis

Bonus Tracks / A Traveler's Companion

"THE PILGRIM ACT IV" (unreleased alternate take) with Ralph Stanley and the Clinch Mountain Boys, Connie Smith, Emmylou Harris, Marty Stuart / **"THAT'LL BE ALL RIGHT WITH ME"** (unreleased) with the Rock & Roll Cowboys: Steve Arnold, Brad Davis, Gary Hogue, Gregg Stocki, with Adam Wood, Jim "Moose" Brown, Marty Stuart / **"BEEN LONELY TOO LONG"** (unreleased Pilgrim project demo) with Richard Bennett, Harry Stinson, Glenn Worf, Barry Beckett, Terri Wilson, Mick Conley, Marty Stuart / **"I THINK WE'RE IN TEXAS"** (unreleased) Manuel and Emmylou Harris / **"SHOUT LITTLE LULIE"** (unreleased) with Ralph Stanley and the Clinch Mountain Boys, Marty Stuart / **"CALL AND RESPONSE"** (unreleased) – Uncle Josh Graves and Marty Stuart / **"EVELINA"** (unreleased) – Uncle Josh Graves and Marty Stuart / **"TENNESSEE WAGONER"** (unreleased) with Earl Scruggs and Stuart Duncan / **"EVEN TRAINS HAVE TO CRY"** (unreleased *Pilgrim* project demo) with the Fabulous Superlatives: Paul Martin, Harry Stinson, Kenny Vaughan, with Gary Carter, Marty Stuart / **"THE VANISHING"** (unreleased *Pilgrim* project demo) – Marty Stuart and Mick Conley

PRODUCED BY: MARTY STUART

ASSISTANT TO MARTY STUART: Maria-Elena Orbea

MIXED AND MASTERED BY: Jamie Tate – The Rukkus Room; Coordination by Dusty Cantrell – The Rukkus Room / Track three recorded – Almo Irving Studio / Track nine recorded – North Star Studios by Mick Conley; Mixed by Mick Conley; Asst. Engineer Al Conley / Track ten recorded – Apartment Number Nine by Mick Conley; Mixed by Mick Conley / Vinyl cut by Joe Nino-Hernes at Sterling Sound, Nashville / Bonus material compiled by John Peets, Q Prime South / Project archivist Jamie Tate

SONGWRITER CREDITS: "THE PILGRIM ACT IV" - Marty Stuart *Marty Party Music (BMI)* / **"THAT'LL BE ALL RIGHT WITH ME"** - Marty Stuart *Marty Party Music (BMI)* / **"BEEN LONELY TOO LONG"** - Marty Stuart & Thom Schuyler *Glitterbilly Music/Irving Music & September Sound Songs (BMI)* / **"I THINK WE'RE IN TEXAS"** - Marty Stuart *Marty Party Music (BMI)* / **"SHOUT LITTLE LULIE"** - Ralph Stanley *Fort Know Music / Trio Music Company (BMI)* / **"CALL AND RESPONSE"** - Marty Stuart *Marty Party Music (BMI)* / **"EVELINA"** – Burkett H. Graves & Jake Lambert *Scruggs Music Inc. (BMI)* / **"TENNESSEE WAGONER"** Traditional, Arranged by Earl Scruggs and Stuart Duncan / **"EVEN TRAINS HAVE TO CRY"** - Marty Stuart *Marty Party Music (BMI)* / **"THE VANISHING"** - Marty Stuart *Marty Party Music (BMI)*

Special thanks to Jamie Tate, who lovingly guarded all of the songs and elements of all things Pilgrim *for the past twenty years. Without his care, this edition of* The Pilgrim *would not exist.*

– Marty Stuart

Jamie Tate's Notes on *The Pilgrim* (2019)

I spent six months recording and mixing *The Pilgrim*. Most of that time was spent following Marty around with microphones for fourteen-plus hours a day, waiting to see which instrument he stopped in front of to play on each song. Some days were fourteen hours, others seemed like thirty-plus hours. Marty's bus was parked at the studio from day one, so he never left. Many of the days ran one into the other, but I was only twenty-four or twenty-five at the time, and at that age you're invincible!

I was tired, but so excited to be working on something this monumental. I was completely committed to making Marty's album the best it could be. It was a long and exhausting process, but we looked forward to each day. None of us knew what to expect. One day we'd have Emmylou Harris stop by to record some vocals. Then Mike Campbell joined us for a few days. As the weeks went on, George Jones, Earl Scruggs, Dolly Parton, Ralph Stanley, John Prine, Travis Tritt, Pam Tillis, Connie Smith, Jim Varney, and Johnny Cash all became a part of *The Pilgrim* parade.

Abtrax, the studio where we worked, wasn't large or luxurious. In fact, it was a former daycare center that had been converted from a funeral home. The main tracking room was where the embalming had taken place. The offices up front were the viewing rooms. The ceilings were only standard height, unlike the more expansive spaces found in most studios. The drums were in a small booth, barely larger than the drum kit. It was all somewhat cramped. The control room was awkward, but the gear was nice. Marty had lamps and enough fabric to cover the walls brought in to make the place look worthy of hosting the recording of such an album as *The Pilgrim*.

I have many happy memories of these sessions. Marty was on a constant creative high. As far as we knew, the songs just existed, but I'm sure Marty sweated blood to create the story, the music, the lyrics, the concept, and the flow of the record. It was a monumental undertaking. But no matter how involved we were in our work, even if Marty was in the middle of a take, when Connie walked in, he would stop whatever he was doing, go over, and give her a hug. That show of affection always made a huge impression on me, and it tells you what kind of person Marty is. Twenty years later, I still think of him making time to hug Connie. That's something I've kept with me and keep alive with my wife and two boys.

The Ralph Stanley "Harlan County" session was special. Marty told me the album would take us through the history of country music, and "Harlan County" was the birth. Not only did it tell us the origins of the album's story, but Ralph Stanley is one of the originators of the genre. I wanted to give the track a more authentic, vintage sound. I set up an old German Telefunken U-47 tube microphone and ran it through a beautiful, vintage Neve mic preamp. One mic. That's it! The musicians had to not only play everything live—perfectly—but they also had to balance themselves against the other players in the room. They each honed in on this musical relationship as the takes went on. I have thirty-six takes of this song where the growth is apparent. The final version on the album is a combination of two takes (thirty-two and thirty-six).

Legendary guitars filled the studio. It was a living museum. Late one night, I set up a few lights and took some pictures of them, which are included in this book.

After the album was finished, Marty and I were back in the studio working on a new project when his phone rang. It was Bob Dylan. I could hear Bob singing "Observations of a Crow." That confirmed what I already knew: that *The Pilgrim* was a unique record with a long reach.

Marty's record label may not have understood what we made, but a stack of glowing reviews the size of a phone book told us we had done something special. Through the years, it seems the audience for this record has grown. I hope this twentieth anniversary edition will give you more insights into this amazing album.

Technical Notes I recorded *The Pilgrim* to a new hard disk recording system called RADAR (Random Access Digital Audio Recorder). This was cutting-edge technology at the time, but is all but forgotten today. Restoring these data tapes proved to be a difficult process. My technical assistant, Joe Nino-Hernes, had to invent a new way to retrieve the information from the RADAR's hard drive so I could load it into the Pro Tools software. Even the company that designed the RADARs had never thought of this new transfer process, which they've now adopted as the best way for their users to recover old recordings. Many thanks to Joe!

To remaster *The Pilgrim* I needed to transfer twenty-six different ninety-minute Digital Audio Tapes into Pro Tools—all in real time! Then I had to edit all the various mixes together in the same way we did during the 1999 mastering session. Some of the edits are combinations of five or six mixes. "John Henry" was a combination of several different takes. I had to listen to everything. That's thirty-nine hours of music! I had to decide which of the dozens of mixes for each song was used for the original CD. After a few weeks I finally had everything in its place—all the hundreds of edits with proper crossfades—and aligned to-the-sample with the original CD. Then came time for the actual mastering, which is adjusting the songs so they all have the same volume and tonality. Hank Williams did a magnificent job mastering the album in 1999, but he has since retired. I hope you like this new remaster, with its shiny new edits, updated EQ, and a definite lack of interest in the Loudness War.

I understood the historical value of these sessions, so I always had a stereo DAT tape ready to record the stereo audio off the console. I didn't want to miss anything. Some of the moments among the bonus material only existed on those DAT tapes, so I have to give my twenty-four-year-old self a twenty-year-delayed high five for preserving those moments.

The bluegrass outtakes were all taken from those session DAT tapes. They are just the stereo output of my console as the band played—no remixing, no overdubs. One hundred percent live.

"That'll Be Alright with Me" was recorded early on in *The Pilgrim* sessions. It was intended to be the first single from the record, and Marty and his band played it during a TV appearance (that I dutifully recorded). We got so far as to record a final vocal for the song before deciding it wouldn't be on the album. When I was thinking about the tracks for this reissue, this was the first song I thought of.

"Lonely Too Long" was recorded in a basement studio in 1997 on another long forgotten (and much maligned) format known as ADAT. It recorded eight tracks of digital audio onto VHS tapes. These machines were slow, clunky, finicky, temperamental, and an unfortunate side note in the evolution of recording technology. The tapes with "Lonely Too Long" were stored in conditions that were not optimal, and the drum tracks are now corrupt. There wasn't more than a bar and a half without a loud glitch, or the drums dropping out completely. I reassembled the track hit by hit. The song was cut without a click track, so the tempo had a humanistic drift to it. Good for music, but bad for reassembling a drum-track-free synch. One thing I will say is the track was well-recorded. Back then, even the guys working in basement studios were top notch.

The Pilgrim is a project that has had to fight for survival. Along with being overlooked when it was released, being taken out of print, and surviving multiple changes of format, I fear the multitracks were lost in the 2008 fire in the Universal vault that claimed more than half a million recordings and movies, including the master tapes for *The Pilgrim*. The multitracks that do still exist are my personal backups. I have all the mixes as well as the entire album safely archived.

November 1,1999

Dear Marty,

Well, it's been a year to the day since we started recording The Pilgrim. I had no idea how I was going to get walloped in the next few months. Not only didn't I sleep in that time but I fainted twice from exhaustion and I now have white hairs growing from my youthful (but out of shape) body. I blame you of course.

Staring at my check from Universal (they neglected to put sufficient postage on the envelope. I had to scurry around to find $.02 in my couch to drop in my mailbox for the postman) that is now framed and hanging on my wall, next to the Marty shrine where I genuflect every hour on the hour, I have fond memories of last year. There's an old saying written on the walls of the Martha Washington Hotel. It reads- "Ten cents is better than no cents if you've got some sense." I don't know what that has to do with what I'm talking about here but I do know that I am sitting in my beautiful house that the Pilgrim helped pay for.

It was all hard work but from the very beginning I knew what you were doing was going to be beyond most artists' capabilities. All the songs on the album are brilliant but the way you put them together and made them flow into a dark and deep story makes the album take on an importance that is bigger than just a collection of tunes. I knew that in twenty years I would still be honored to have my name on this album and would be one of the things I'm proudest of.

I was always eager to go to the studio (if eager means barely awake) because of what I was learning every day. I loved listening to your stories about all the people I admire and about the history of your guitars and hearing you play them just to show off to Connie was a real treat. That right there should be an album and I still think you should write a book and put all your stories in it. Release it under the name Stuart Martin so you won't get sued.

People fall in love with the record (as I did). I get quite a bit of you when ever I go into Tower Records. They've been playing The Pilgrim CD in store since its release. At first I thought it was just my entrance music but I later found out that several of the employees (none of which say they like country music) accidentally heard your record and recognized its brilliance. One girl said The Crow was the best song she'd ever heard. Not a week goes by when I don't get a "WOW! You worked on the Pilgrim," from someone going in or out of the studio.

You should be proud of the work you've done. This album will be the reason why someone gets into music. We all have our musical foundation from which we drawn a lifetime of inspiration and this will be just that to many people.

I am very proud and honored to have been a part of The Pilgrim. Thank you fo everything you've taught me.

Regards, affection, admiration and, if you want to throw in a few superlatives o your own, I have no objection.

Yours,

Jamie Tate

Jamie Tate

Jamie Tate Archives